THE *MOMENTUM* FACTOR

How to Keep Your Team Motivated Through Building
Purpose, Direction, and Trust

TAMILYN BANNO

TamilynBanno.com
Tami@LetLeadershipLive.com

Cover Image: frankrohde / 123RF Stock Photo
Editor: Sarah Lingley Williams (lingleyediting.com)
Logo Design: Joseph Banno (jjbcuts@yahoo.com)
Author Photo: Renee Mayer

ISBN: 1507650809
ISBN-13: 978-1507650806

ENDORSEMENTS

"This helpful, practical book shows how to use a leadership retreat to build a peak performance team that really gets results."

Brian Tracy, Best Selling Author, Success Expert, and CEO of Brian Tracy International

"There is a devastating divide between the need for great leaders and the willingness of organizations to invest in training and supporting them. And even when they are willing to invest, they almost always leave out the one method that creates the greatest 'leader-shift' possible. While building forward momentum by incorporating retreats may seem counter-intuitive, in The Momentum Factor, *Tamilyn Banno takes the lessons she learned on her journey from corporate leadership to inexperienced sales manager to top sales leader in her organization, and distills that lifetime of learning into a replicatable method for fast tracking your leaders by getting them to slow down and connect."*

Dixie Gillaspie, Coach/Consultant, Author of *Just Blow It Up: Firepower for Living an Unlimited Life*

"Tamilyn's message about Leadership is not only refreshing and inspiring, but also thought-provoking and relevant in today's society. A must read for any leader who wants to make a difference with their sales team!"

Deb Cottle, Motivational Speaker/Coach, Co-Author of *Success Simplified* with Dr. Stephen Covey, *Roadmap to Success*, and creator of the 4STEP GUTS FORMULA.

"Having served in the Army's Special Forces, been a Chief of Police and Special Agent for the Federal Government, I have seen both sides of supervision and the complexities involved. I think that Tamilyn has captured the philosophy of getting people to want to work with you instead of having work for you. This book is a primer, not only for first time supervisors, but for long time supervisors looking for fresh ideas. Good reading!"

Gary Morefield
Special Agent (Retired) U.S.
Treasury

"A truly insightful and action-inspiriting book! Tamilyn Banno has clearly illustrated that the essence of leadership is influence which is a direct reflection of our own authenticity. She leads us step-by-step through her MMPP Leadership Retreat model for creating real momentum and results."

Kathy Zader, President, Go-Giver International

DEDICATION

To the leaders who serve, everywhere—Let Leadership Live!

ACKNOWLEDGMENTS

I could never have completed this 2-year project without help. If you didn't contribute to a specific chapter in this book then you helped me create, formulate, and articulate the words within the pages through conversations you thought were random, or by providing me with inspiration in ways you never realized.

Gabriela Banno, Tamilyn C. Banno, Alessandra Banno, Joseph Banno, Daniella Banno, Maria Banno:

MUAH!

Jan Drawe, Geoffrey Berwind, Christopher Mayer, Michelle Mayer, Renee Mayer, Dustin Mayer, Adrienne Jasiczek, Lisa Mayer, Kates Smiles, Donna Banno, Kate Stuart, Gary and Linda Morefield, Debbie Sneyd, Jade Venovich Wagenbach, Tim Seyda, Margaret Naughton, Brenda Goett, Angela Robinson, Margo Heintz, Henry Holling, Dixie Gillaspie, Bob Burg, Steve Harrison, Marianne Friedlund, Kim Leider, Carolyn Anderson, Jamaria Martins, Cheryl Bjerke, Jules Abbott, Veronica Otten-Goldman, Francisca Kear, Colette French, Kathy Burke, Debby Gibson, Dina Vardal, Wendy Thomas-Williams, and Lisa Buben.

To my editor, Sarah Lingley Williams, you're an amazing and talented gift. Thank you!

To Joseph, my biggest "Tink."
Happy 30th Anniversary!
All My Love,
-t

Momentum is based on your lead, and determined by the art of your interpersonal skills.

The *Momentum* Factor

TAMILYN BANNO

You are the most amazingly natural leader. Your presence is Motivation in itself and the reason we have become leaders. Your smile and energy give others the sense that anything can be accomplished. Just look how many people you work with who are accomplishing life goals above and beyond what they ever could have imagined. The skills from this experience will carry us on to our next ventures and throughout our lives.

Veronica Otten-Goldman (Illinois), Entrepreneur, Retreat Attendee

TAMILYN BANNO

CONTENTS

THE BEGINNING JOURNAL

In your own words, define leadership.

_____

_____

_____

_____

Is there a leader or mentor you admire? Describe his/her leadership style.

_____

_____

_____

_____

_____

_____

_____

Describe the leader you want to become.

_____

_____

_____

_____

_____

What do you value most about your position?

What do you value least about your position?

_____

_____

_____

_____

_____

_____

_____

_____

Recall a time when you sensed an effortless flow of teamwork in your role as a leader. Describe what happened as if it's in the present time. What personal strengths are shining forth? What are you doing, as a leader, to encourage and inspire others? What changes in or with your department or team are happening because of it?

_____

_____

_____

_____

_____

_____

_____

_____

_____

_____

_____

_____

_____

Have you ever been on a retreat—either work-related or personal? If so, describe the format and what positive or negative effects transpired between you and your team after the event.

_____

_____

_____

_____

_____

_____

_____

_____

_____

_____

_____

_____

_____

_____

PREFACE

The outline for this book is based on a personal business/life journey I began a few years ago. I held a leadership position in the sales industry and was frustrated with the stalemate of team production numbers. As a determined leader, I wanted the number one position and I wanted it yesterday. I worked hard; I *deserved* it yesterday!

At the same time, I questioned the direction of my life. 'Am I in the right business? I'm working endless hours; where's the shining outcome? Why can't I *receive* the gifts and success that everyone talks about when *giving* so much, all of the time?' I wasn't feeling a sense of purpose or fulfillment. Although I attended many leadership seminars just to keep my heart in the game, I yearned for something else—something more— that I couldn't seem to find.

Then I met Bob.

We first met over the internet and exchanged a few emails. I explained my dilemma and he was patient to listen. His advice was forward, yet friendly. The deeper my questions became, the more wisdom he provided: "Receiving is the natural result of giving. In fact, every giving can happen only because it is also receiving."

During the course of our emails, I was reserved in believing the conversations were actually written by the speaker and author Mr. Bob Burg, himself. In fact, he cyber-laughed when I questioned his authenticity. In the end, however, I decided to attend his upcoming conference which, in turn, was to be the biggest game changer of my life.

Bob is in the business of building relationships. A part of his life-specialty is his alluring disposition to connect with others and the ability to bring value to their business through his Five Laws to Stratospheric Success.

Years prior, Bob and one of his friends, John David Mann, wrote a best seller book about a "Powerful Business Idea" called *The Go-Giver*. I enjoyed the story and was satisfied knowing my personality followed the concept. But it wasn't until I met Bob in person that I understood it wasn't a concept; being a Go-Giver is a way of life. You're either a Go-Giver, or you're not.

The Go-Giver story is about Joe, a 'go-*getter*' who's frustrated because no matter how fast or hard he works, his goals always seem to be further away. When he's desperate to meet his monthly sales quota, he seeks advice from Pindar, a legendary and wise consultant.

Pindar introduces Joe to several go-*givers* who strategically teach him the Five Laws to Stratospheric Success. The Laws shift Joe's focus from *getting* to *giving*. When adding value to others by putting their interests first, it opens up the power to receive.

"I need you to agree that you will test every Law I show you by actually trying it out. Not by thinking about it, not by talking about it, but by applying it in your life." —*The Go-Giver*

As a result of Mr. Burg's conference, I studied the Five Laws to Stratospheric Success with a certified Go-Giver coach. There is a difference between believing in the concept and intentionally applying the Laws. Once I consciously engaged in them, it opened the portal to receive, and the momentum of my business soared. In fact, I went from #3 in the company to #1 in 30 days!

Although I do not explain the Five Laws in detail, there are notations throughout my book where they served me well. This purpose is to add more value to your reading in hopes that you, too, may read *The Go-Giver* and apply the Laws to your own life.

After all, I can't be the only 'Joe' searching for the ultimate success.

The Go-Giver
By Bob Burg and John David Mann

The Five Laws to Stratospheric Success

The Law of Value
Your true worth is determined by how much more you give in value than you take in payment.

The Law of Compensation
Your income is determined by how many people you serve and how well you serve them.

The Law of Influence
Your influence is determined by how abundantly you place other peoples' interest first.

The Law of Authenticity
The most valuable gift you have to offer is yourself.

The Law of Receptivity
The key to effective giving is to stay open to receiving.

INTRODUCTION: LET LEADERSHIP LIVE!

I can't paint a pretty picture—leadership is in a flat line crisis. For decades, business and psychological researchers have been analyzing the working relationships between employees and their respective organizations. These annual surveys provide companies with insights into employee engagement in the workplace; unfortunately, the levels of disengagement continue to be staggering. Employees around the world are dissatisfied, and even hate their jobs. According to Gallup's 2013 State of the American Workplace Report, slightly over 10% of workers around the world are reported engaged; actively connecting and contributing to their job. This means nearly 90% of employees are *not* engaged; frustrated, distressed, and most likely working in your department. "Houston, we have a problem."

Since the global recession in 2007, the American workforce continues to struggle with unemployment, spending cuts, and employee disengagement. A direct deposit of stress and fear is committed to filling our lives. Our mental and physical health plummets, resulting in depression, anxiety, burn-out, and more. When our financial and personal securities are at risk, our work performance is, too.

Disengaged employees who emotionally disconnect are less likely to be productive. They can affect product quality and even contribute to carelessness. More than ever, organizations need leaders to rally their troops. Unfortunately, only a fraction of leaders know how.

The truth is, people aren't inspired anymore. Employees are tired, unappreciated, and they lack passion. In the same way, leaders are also tired, overextended, and have lost their direction; to make matters worse, leaders have lost their influence. Their spirit is hanging on by a clinging chad; grabbing at random, half-hearted motivational attempts in order to keep a team moving.

In this frightening reality, we need an emotional rescue. We need good leaders to be great by taking the reins and changing the direction of engagement. We need strong pathfinders; leaders who will dig deep, make a commitment, and help revitalize visions.

Leaders in any capacity or level have the power to inspire and motivate the individuals they work with, but they don't, or they can't, figure out how to use their influence and ask, "Why would anyone want to follow me?" Sometimes, through no fault of their own, they are pushed into their position without any insight into what it means to lead and wonder, "Why isn't anyone following me?" They try to engage their team only to experience frustrating and hopeless results.

During my tenure as a top director, I struggled with energizing both individuals and myself. I experienced the discombobulated team, I ran out of incentives and magic tricks to propel production. Through those very difficult years, I doubted my skills, and was never able to master the flow of continuous momentum that all leaders crave; until, that is, I discovered my purpose and the deeper reasons for why I lead. This discovery was invaluable, and continues to affect my business and life today.

Leadership development courses come in all shapes and sizes from In-services, Webinars, Teleseminars, to various on-site and off-site conferences. The discovery of my purpose, and how this merges with the company during an off-site retreat, was profoundly insightful. This clarity led to higher aspirations and, ultimately, triggered the momentum of my team.

Hundreds of books crowded my bookshelves, but not one mentioned *the retreat* as a blueprint to success. Yet, it is *the* piece that sparked the energy I needed and engaged my team to becoming the top producers in the company. With this valuable experience, I couldn't wait to share it with others, but with so much dissention in the workplace, is it sufficient? A retreat can spark momentum, but is it enough to rejuvenate the declining state of leadership? Unfortunately, leadership development is the one piece of continuing education that's easily cut from company budgets. Though devastating results have been proven with its absence, more and more companies and individuals in upper management still choose to be blinded to its true merit. Just over 10% of employees across the world are engaged…come on! This failing statistic cannot be ignored.

Can a retreat change the declining state of leadership? The answer is *yes,* when leaders truly understand the power of purpose, direction, and trust, and how they factor into building momentum. Momentum is the key to successful motivation.

During a retreat this energy is released and as a result, motivation and production soar.

The reality is, leadership is crumbling and leaders are the only ones who can put it back together. Retreats will only happen when leaders once again respect their value and the value of others, when their faith in leadership turns fearless, and when they desire to deepen their gift of leadership in order to serve and strengthen others.

Whether you manage an entire organization, a department, team, or one person, I hope through reading this book you will grasp a deeper understanding of great leadership, you will lead with admirable influence, and you will organize powerful annual retreats. There is a natural disaster in the workplace, and the only way out is through the heart of leadership.

Let's start something! Let's revive the workplace, and Let Leadership Live!

PART ONE

Life as a Leader

TAMILYN BANNO

WE LEAK

You already know how to be a great leader! A long time ago you were given the tools required to fulfill your role, but hey, we all *leak* now and then. Blame the "collywobbles"; they're the culprit.

Morning, noon and night we add more to our plate. A pile of procrastination sits next to the heartache of overwhelm; the helpings of misguided influencers blend with the heap of self-doubt. Steadily, we put pressure on the leadership brakes; we slow down our momentum, yet still we hope to move forward. Every time we gently press on that pedal, it gets harder and harder to release.

In the meantime, the lack of greater leadership haunts us. Our employees are disgruntled, and whispering hearsay behind our back. We find it easier to close our door than to invite in a confrontation. Anxiety and uncertainty twist deep in our gut, and we allow this fear to cloud our ability to think and act boldly. We have a bad case of the "collywobbles," and they begin to leak all over the place.

In an insanely fast paced world, this fear and loss of leadership identity gives bigger strength to outside forces. We face more giants than David and can only find tiny pebbles with which to fill our slingshot. We bandage our wounds and hope they heal on their own, but we know they won't. As leaders, we run in all directions trying to fulfill the needs of many others, all the while ignoring our own. We're overwhelmed, tired, and too gun-shy to make courageous moves. Even when we become a victim of our circumstances, they still require *us* to be the hero.

For many years, terrifying numbers of disengaged employees have been representing businesses across the globe. According to Gallup's 2013 Report, 87% of the people employed today are disconnected and even hate their jobs. This means that for nearly a decade, only a fraction of people have been applying their best effort in *your* organization or department. If this isn't scary enough, guess who's to blame? *The leader.*

As a leader, YOU are accountable for the people under your direction. You are the host serving inspiration and communication, and the one motivating them into production. The ability to turn your vision into a productive outcome is always a challenge. Leaders need an active team in order to produce, but first, leaders need a team who wants to listen in order to take action. If your team is not moving or listening, what are you communicating?

Sally Hogshead, marketing guru and bestselling author of *Fascinate*, focuses her work on first impressions. "As humans, we fascinate one another each time we interact, with every syllable of our voices, every waft of our scents, every flicker of our expressions...If we use our natural cues, people will join us. If we don't, they'll walk away."

Most people in the workforce do not want to be at work, let alone *work* at work. Sure, your department might be getting things done, but only with half a heart and half of what they're capable of doing. The time to turn engagement around is long overdue, and you hold the natural energy to *fascinate* them!

According to the 2013 U.S. Bureau of Labor Statistics, we spend over half of our waking hours at work, not including preparation and travel time. If we spend most of our lives working, then it only makes sense to devote more time to building the character and strengths of the individual. The *Momentum Model of Leadership Development* (discussed further in Part I) illustrates how a team can swiftly move forward; it's a natural, effortless flow of energy that guides a team to sustainable success. The energy of momentum is streamed *through the leader.*

Defining your *why*—your vision, your purpose—enables you to speak credibly and to inspire others to know theirs, too. As a leader, your gift is to captivate and encourage others to exercise their strongest quality, or highest value, and it begins with understanding your strengths and desires first.

Leaders who are in balance with their vison and the vision of the company have a clear direction toward their goals. However, many managers dive into a leadership position clueless which way to go. Interestingly, according to TINYpulse 2013 survey, only 42% of these people know their organization's mission statement. It's difficult enough jumping into the middle of an ongoing project, yet realistically, that's where most leaders are plopped. In addition, plenty of leadership levels are temporary, a stepping stone to another position. Subsequently, minimal commitment on their part is offered, at best. The Momentum

Model helps every leader in any organization learn how to ignite a power play, if he or she is willing.

Another critical issue facing organizations is their ability or inability to develop future leaders. In a recent article written by Adam Vaccaro, *So Much Potential, So Little Investment; Why Great Talent Languishes* (inc.com, 2014), he cites interesting survey results from Gap International: Corporate Executives' Views on Leadership, Employee Performance, and Innovation.

> *"Executives overwhelmingly agree that talent can make or break a company; yet only a minority actually say they invest in leadership development programs. How important is maximizing a company's talent? Very, said 85 percent of execs surveyed. In addition, 83 percent said the same of empowering employees to succeed.*
>
> *If it's really that important, why aren't more companies investing in leadership training programs? Gap International CEO Pontish Yeramyan says that the ROI is not clear, so companies don't invest much effort or money into them. Before companies can invest serious energy into leadership development, they must put plans in place that guarantee strong outcomes of the programs, she says."*

Seriously? Knowing it's the right move to invest in leadership development, *yet not choosing to pursue the golden ticket to deeper employee engagement* even though it reflects the growth and success of the organization? How is this plausible? My ROI with leadership retreats have always hit the top of the charts.

Leadership is *real*; leaders motivate *real* people to increase a company's *real* value. With the toiling undercurrents of the economic climate, leaders leak and become weak. Annual retreats strengthen leaders. They are the missing link to better management and growth, but not every CEO sees deep enough into his organization to give it credence, and most importantly, not every retreat is the same. The quality of a retreat can be as misguided as a misdirected leader. The Momentum Model credits the MMPP format (Maintenance, Motivation, Purpose, and Plan) as the tipping point to higher team engagement. (This is discussed further in Part II.) The MMPP model engages individuals while maximizing group potential.

When leaders have the opportunity to come together and share stories, challenges, and ideas, they align their focus with the company's mission—their surge can cause a power-outage! Leadership retreats provide the perfect atmosphere to move leaders to a more connected and productive organization. Momentum sparks and as a result, teams are fired-up to move. Without teamwork, there's little hope for significant increase.

Leadership *matters*; its presence influences individuals throughout most of their adult life's journey. People are hungry to be valued, to belong, to be a part of something, and they look toward leaders to show them the way. *How are you fascinating your team? Where are you taking them?* If you've never asked yourself these questions, or don't know the answers, keep reading.

Leadership must be *challenged*. Leaders don't wait for upper management to move people; *they* move people! Leaders don't wait to be fascinated, *they* fascinate people! If it's up to YOU to organize and host your own retreat, then schedule one! Your team will be well on their way to higher engagement and productivity.

This isn't rocket science; it's elementary. Remember, you already possess the attributes to lead. Release the anxiety collywobbles that are holding down the brake pedal, and guide with confidence. Allow me to share with you the missing information from other leadership books that took my team from #3 in the company to #1 in 30 days!

WHAT MAKES A GOOD LEADER GREAT

The origin of the word 'leader' is Old English and according to the Collins Dictionary, "one who leads." In the context of this book, a leader is a person who guides and inspires. Here are some of the characteristics that describe great leaders:

SOUND JUDGMENT: A great leader assesses situations shrewdly and is willing to accept challenges with confidence.

COMMUNICATOR: A great leader communicates, trains, and builds relationships using a variety of media outlets.

RELIANT: A great leader is available and actively engages in teamwork.

PURPOSE: A great leader clarifies his or her personal purpose and knows how it merges with that of the company.

REACH THROUGH ORGANIZATION: A great leader will utilize company development opportunities and communicate with other leaders to gain and share wisdom and strengths.

HUMBLE: A great leader is humble, honest, and not boastful. He/she is respectful, and not arrogant.

A SENSE OF HUMOR: A great leader enjoys life and does

not take everything so seriously.

EMOTIONAL INTELLIGENCE: A great leader places himself/herself inside the emotions of another person's feelings and has the ability to merge and connect on an emotional level.

ADAPT: Change happens, always. A great leader does not impulsively react, but instead focuses on the benefits of the change.

AUTHENTIC: A great leader leads from the inside out and genuinely motivates for the good of the people.

VISION: A great leader is in tune to where the team is headed and is not afraid to recalculate the direction.

MAINTENANCE: A great leader maintains a personal balance and takes time-out for physical and mental fitness.

MENTOR: A great leader is active in continuing education; he/she seeks out mentors and is a mentor to others.

DEFINING CLEAR GOALS: A great leader defines specific goals, which allows the team to visualize the outcome.

STRENGTH FINDER: A great leader will pursue the right people for a particular job or project, utilizing individual strengths in order to reach specific goals.

What other characteristics make a good leader great?

_____

_____

_____

_____

_____

_____

_____

_____

_____

_____

TAMILYN BANNO

WHY LEADERS FAIL

More and more leaders are losing the drive to stimulate their department or team. Uninspiring leaders who try to motivate employees…well, you can imagine how that turns out. If the fire isn't burning on the inside of the leader, then motivating a team simply can't happen.

LACK OF SOUND JUDGMENT: An uninspiring leader doesn't use logic or common sense or is too timid to take risks.

LACK OF COMMUNICATION: An uninspiring leader does not engage in one-on-one training, clarify projects, or attempt at build relationships.

SELF-RELIANT: An uninspiring leader does not delegate projects, but instead does all the work.

NO PURPOSE: An uninspiring leader has no direction and no passion.

POLITICAL GAIN: An uninspiring leader shows subtle acts of manipulation for personal gain.

LACK OF EMPATHY: An uninspiring leader does not take the time to show a genuine interest in another person.

JUDGMENTAL: An uninspiring leader is quick to draw

conclusions; he/she lacks humility and respect.

TOO RIGID: An uninspiring leader is continually stressed out and takes life way too seriously.

REFUSE TO ADAPT: An uninspiring leader is too defiant to change; he/she is quick to voice negative opinions and takes too long to move a team forward.

LOSS OF VISION: An uninspiring leader is a disengaged leader; he/she has lost heart, passion, and enthusiasm toward the team, or toward a specific goal.

DISTRUST: An uninspiring leader lacks integrity and does not stand by his/her word.

WEAK: An uninspiring leader is a tired leader; he/she is strung out, out of balance, and refuses to take a time-out for rejuvenation.

ARROGANT: An uninspiring leader thinks he/she knows it all; refuses to grow or develop his/her skills.

NO GOALS: An uninspiring leader is without direction; he/she has no idea where the team is headed.

List other reasons why leaders fail.

_____

_____

_____

_____

_____

_____

_____

_____

_____

_____

Leadership is suffering and as a result, so are the people leaders manage. The fact is, there are people who should not lead. I've had both Jekyll and Hyde supervisors, but the ones that lack good leadership skills have actually made me a better leader.

It's important to keep your own leadership skills in tact; key in on individual strengths, then make every effort to acknowledge them.

I do my best to follow this rule by monopolizing on my teams' strengths and showing my appreciation for their contributions.

Don't be a victim of poor leadership; be the professional who turns it around.

Sergeant Dina Vardal (Illinois)

PART TWO

Pushing for Power

OR

Pulling for Purpose, Direction, and Trust

PURPOSE

TURTLE SOUP, ANYONE?:
How To Slow Down in a Fast-Paced World

Recently, I was flipping through the TV channels and landed on the Slowsky's, you know, the annoying slow-turtle couple on the DSL commercials. They prefer to use a lackadaisical internet server and for most humans, it's agonizing to watch. As quick as my own connection is, if I have to wait a few extra seconds for a page to load, I dig deep and let out a bellowing, "UGH!" Can't anybody crack through the turtles' shells and convince them faster is better?

Despite the Slowsky's slow-paced comforts, technology continues to accelerate. Back in 1947, Edwin Land excited the world with his advancement of print photography. Land's company, the Polaroid Corporation, changed the traditional chemical processing from paper directly onto the film, giving birth to the instant camera. For the first time, we held pictures in our hands within minutes after taking the snapshot. Today, we share life instantly all over the world through the technology of camera phones and social media. As soon as we post an image, we're snapping another one. If we captured a drunken-stupor-like expression in a sober moment, no problem, we can delete it and take another one in the blink of an eye. (Yep, I really like the faster side of things!)

The desire for instant gratification isn't new, but the need for speed has become an addiction. Though technology has become extremely efficient, we're still not satisfied. In the instagram of life, we want more results faster; lose ten pounds in *two days*, master Candy Crush *in seconds*, or become a Fortune 500 company *overnight*. We spend our time and resources learning how to do things at a screaming pace, but sadly, we're not paying attention to what we're becoming in the process.

In business, the role of leadership is more important today than ever before. Organizations compete for customers, and in this world of desiring immediate success, a vital component is neglected. Managers and leaders push for production in order to keep their jobs, but at what risk?

According to the April 2014 U.S. Bureau of Labor Statistics, the unemployment rate has steadily increased since 2008. As corners get cut and job opportunities fall, upper management bleeds more out of fewer employees. The corporate atmosphere turns defensive and departments react from fear of failing, foregoing a virtue here and there. Without much thought, we rush for the outcome, risking product quality, customer loyalty, and our own reputation for goodwill in order to reach monthly quotas. The bottom line is about production, but sometimes we take the bottom line and make it all about our top. Sometimes we turn all our focus onto the numbers, with little consideration of who's producing them, and thereby abandon the purpose of a leader.

During my twelve years as a senior director in the sales industry, my continuing education was molded by the research and development from some of the top authors and professors in the field, yet every leadership book I've ever read is missing the biggest piece to employee engagement— the crossroads where instant-mania and a turtle's pace meet.

Across the globe, influential executives, CEO's, and entrepreneurs slow down and participate in their own innovation retreats, grounding their purpose, gaining inspiration, and renewing their business vision. The role of a leader is vitally important; the responsibility to increase production depends on understanding the company's vision, in addition to motivating employees. Unless there's a genuine respect between the two, an organization is not prepared for increase.

Believe it or not, the Slowsky's had a character blog where everything *slow* was celebrated. Is it possible to create a slow-space in a fast-paced world? Instant gratification has its merits, but when it comes to people, there's nothing better than the process of appreciation. In order for companies to receive the full benefits of a synergistic system, it's necessary to implement new behaviors at the leadership level. Leaders are driven by the success of their upper management, inspiring VP's and CEO's. Their own leadership retreat is equally important.

Retreats help leaders lead more effectively. They are the missing link to an engaged workplace, which results in an increase of production, profitability, and gratifying customers. When leaders take quality time to focus on both their personal growth and that of the company, they will make a positive difference in every way.

Perhaps in this world where faster is better, we should

approach things more consciously. Annual leadership retreats open the flow of engagement and purpose, which ensures growth. Take a few days to regroup, refocus, revisit visions, and let's put a welcome mat out for the Slowsky's.

> *"Those people who develop the ability to continuously acquire new and better forms of knowledge that they can apply to their work and to their lives will be the movers and shakers in our society for the indefinite future." —Brian Tracy*

Imagine taking a weekend trip—an escape from all your daily demands. Where would you go? What would you be doing right now?

_____

_____

_____

_____

_____

_____

_____

_____

_____

_____

_____

_____

_____

Taking part in Tami's leadership retreats was truly a life-altering and eye-opening experience. As a senior leader on her team, I felt completely valued, understood and appreciated. As a mentor to my own leaders, the realization of just how important they were in motivating and building momentum among their team members was invaluable.

I had the honor of participating in two of Tami's retreats, the value I took away was two-fold. First, I believe a retreat is a celebration of success and accomplishments for each individual. Everyone wants to be celebrated and recognized for his/her hard work and dedication. The retreat did just that; Tami celebrated us from the moment the invitation was sent right into the Maintenance aspect of the retreat. What better way to know we are valued then to experience some pampering while being reminded to take care of ourselves. Maintenance truly makes us understand just how important we are to the leader, to the team, to ourselves, and to the people we love.

Second, the other three aspects of the retreat: Motivation, Purpose and Plan, add value in terms of gaining and building momentum—not just individually, but in realizing we are part of a team and a bigger plan. Every outing and every activity was so carefully thought through, reminding us of our importance and bringing us back to our "why." The retreat was fuel for the soul—keeping everyone motivated while continuing along the same successful path and at the same time, dreaming bigger dreams and reaching for bigger goals.

We all walked away armed with ideas, renewed energy and most importantly, support. The bond and sisterhood that developed is immeasurable—a driving force to continue our journey.

After the retreat we headed back to reality with a refreshed sense of purpose. We had great plans that had been mapped out for another year of success that were built on a truly motivating experience.

Kim Leider (Illinois), Personal Fashion Stylist, Retreat Attendee

TAMILYN BANNO

DIRECTION

MAGICAL MANAGERS:
The Power House of the Organization

Leaders are masters of employee engagement. They are the conduit between upper management and employees, and encompass titles such as supervisor, manager, front manager, department head, etc. Regardless of their level of leadership, they are the gatekeepers to a company's production.

Organizations succeed through the best work that their team members provide. According to Michael Brenner, (*ForbesBrandVoice, March 2014*), and Gallup's 2013 State of the Global Workplace report, "When organizations successfully engage their customers and their employees, they experience a 240% boost in performance-related business outcomes compared with an organization with neither engaged employees nor engaged customers." Employees who connect emotionally with customers directly impact productivity and profitability.

Leaders are the magical managers who harness this power of inspiration. Leaders who focus on employee strengths and positive characteristics engage the employees. People are happy, and companies are happy—and profitable. When leaders increase the energy of the department, they change the direction of the workplace into a supportive environment. When both attitudes and conditions become favorable, employees actually enjoy their jobs.

> *"We erect fences in our leadership styles, shutting ourselves away from the imaginations of each other. We need to clearly articulate that a collaborative and engaged culture can and will instill openness, imagination, growth, and promotion of ideas and innovation. We are not here to see through each other, we're here to see each other through."* —Dan Ponterfract, Flat Army.

Collaboration is essential for a prosperous business. When working at Pixar, Steve Jobs held mandatory meetings, dragging designers, programmers, and producers to the atrium of the building. His leadership styles forced isolated geniuses to come together in thought-provoking sessions to learn, connect, and create in a group setting.

Over the years, a variety of leadership styles have governed departments. These unique traits were learned from appropriate generations. Today, a new challenge exists. With younger employees reaching new levels of management, there's another leadership style being added to the mix. We are about to unite three eclectic personalities in the same workplace. Companies world-wide are writing about the fearful direction of this new leadership cocktail.

Baby Boomers, born around 1946-1964, are defined by their strong values and hard work. They believe in working their way up the ladder, and they hold a high regard to hierarchy. They are loyal employees who are extremely committed, and most often stay in the same company during their career.

While many Boomers head for retirement, the core of the generation, Gen X, developed their own personality traits. Gen X, born around 1965-1977, is independent, resourceful, and has an ambitious thirst for knowledge. These individuals want to provide meaningful work, and contribute to humanity. They have strong family values, and prefer work-from-home careers.

Millennials, or Gen Y, born around 1978-1987, want a voice in the workplace, but will generally not climb any corporate ladders. They are driven less by money and more by accomplishments. Millennials want to know the work they provide is valuable to the company and to the environment. They want to express their own creativity, and desire to be personally coached or mentored. (This characteristic likely stems from the cutting edge of technology that was literally put in their laps.) They are swift to learn and because of little job security today, they will move through a variety of organizations during their career.

Are three heads better than one? Caterpillar Inc. is among many companies facing generational confrontation. CAT employs approximately 125,341 people around the world. In the coming year, a vast number of executives will head for retirement, and a new, younger breed will move into their positions. Three generations with different value systems are about to collide. Or are they?

Caterpillar University reaches through their organization with an in-house training development program for all employees at every level. They also contract colleges such as U of I, Duke, and MIT, and utilize other resources and retreat centers that are known for developing emerging leaders.

"CAT takes great pride in their training and development," says Henry Holling, retired VP Manager of Caterpillar

Foundation and Manager Social Responsibility Initiatives. "Good management and leadership go hand and hand, it's imbedded in our culture. Our training is continuous; it doesn't stop when you become a VP or a group president." Mr. Holling quotes Lao Tzu, the ancient Chinese Philosopher: "As for the best leaders, the people do not notice their existence. The next best, the people honor and praise. The next, the people fear; and the next, the people hate...when the best leader's work is done the people say, 'We did it ourselves!'" Creative leadership, despite the generation gaps, is the CAT approach. It begins with the hiring process, and never ends.

The Harvard Business Review posted an article in 2013 highlighting a new direction in communication for merging the gaps. PepsiCo implemented a program called Conn3ct. This organization of Millennial members (Gen Y) establishes connections across the company. They are able to reach out to veteran leaders and offer their perspectives from culture to technology and insight on how to recruit the next generation. According to Paul Marchand, SVP of Field HR at PepsiCo, "This young talent pool continues to support recruiting events for new young professionals to enter the company, helps in product development and marketing initiatives, and contributes to improving the overall work-life balance of employees." By understanding how to work and direct the Gen Y employees, companies will retain them and have the opportunity to train their own future leaders. If not, they will be lost and hired by competitors.

Human connections are more important than ever. If we don't stop to recognize the importance of human engagement then we're contradicting ourselves about the value of leadership and how it influences others. Humanity drives businesses and without it, there is no one to lead.

An interview with Lindsey Pollak, author of "Becoming the Boss (Generation Y: From Team Members to Leaders, August 2014)" in *Psychology Today*, Nancy Ancowitz asks advice for Gen Y readers to help them grow from team members to leaders. Lindsey responds, "The most important strategies are to research the VIP extensively before reaching out (e.g., read their blog, follow them on Twitter, read their LinkedIn profile, read articles about them) and reach out in a polite, professional way that shows you've done your homework on this person." Lindsey adds, "They (Gen Y) have tremendous potential, but need guidance on 'soft skills' such as face-to-face communication, work ethic, and professional patience."

There's a little bit of heaven on earth that I indulge in when I visit Amelia Island, Florida; Bar Zin. This little, cozy, neighborhood American bistro is locally owned and managed by Tim Seyda. The food is incredible and the ambiance comforting, but it's the warm and friendly wait staff that draws me in time and again. Each person is inviting, kind, and respectful to guests, and even to their co-workers. Over the course of my many visits and conversations with the servers, I always mention how much they seem to enjoy their work. Each one of them responds, "It's because of Tim."

In response to my inquiry to Tim, he says, "I simply treat people the way I would want to be treated; open and honest. I hire good people from the start with good attitudes, happy and positive. I can teach people customer service, but I can't train people how to smile." Most of Tim's servers fall into the

Millennial generation, and he observes how he connects with them in order to build quality relationships. "Young people, even young managers, have a difficult time communicating. They take every conversation as a confrontation so you have to work with that knowledge and move forward." Tim manages with the 'Top 3 - Bottom 3' skillset: when an employee requires Tim's direction for improvement, he starts a conversation. He begins with three compliments on his or her work performances and then leads into the three weaknesses he wants him or her to improve upon. Tim finishes the conversation with, "And I'm going to help you with these."

"I wouldn't do anything that I don't ask of my team. I clear tables, tend bar, take reservations, and roll up my sleeves to wash dishes. Funny, but not too long ago a couple of employees actually handed me a portion of their tips! Of course, I didn't accept."

What employee has ever wanted to pay his or her manager?

Comprehending individual leadership styles is critical during this transition between generations. When the purpose of leadership is performance, and the first struggle is the complexity of communication, there's an added dimension of stress on the leader. However, accepting the differences and focusing on connecting individual strengths are the proactive approach to great leadership.

Angela Robinson, Assistant Chief Deputy Clerk to Cook County Government, oversees ten managers and ninety employees, with a combination from each generation. "Success is not about us, but about serving others successfully. To ensure the office runs efficiently I have to orchestrate my management team to manage their own staff and workflow, while providing excellent customer service. To be a successful leader, you have to clarify goals, focus on strengths, know how to communicate, listen, encourage, support, and to administer corrections at the appropriate time and manner. Leadership has its challenges today, but it has to come with a 'no nonsense-be accountable,' attitude."

More than ever, managers need to be magical. They need to dig deep and pull out their best traits to serve and advance their team. Divisional conflict among leaders has happened in the past and will continue with the next generation; the key is to provide direction and quality time for communication. In order to ground the company's vision, leaders must implement unique training and maintain a clear path to engagement; leadership support is mandatory.

Transferring a training opportunity into the atmosphere of an offsite retreat heightens individual learning skills. This concentration of personal development is enlightening. It's the crescendo of the musical composition, the climax of a Broadway play, the 'Aha' moment of realization. When leaders of all generations collaborate in a concentrated group setting, exciting interrelationships and innovations develop.

Three days of a well-balanced weekend is the guaranteed game changer in your business. Yes, only three days! For years I've been attending and hosting my own retreats, and each one has had an impact on my life and in my business. When leaders come together, letters don't count; for Gen A B C or X Y Z, success is inevitable.

In preparation for a retreat, gather a list of your team leaders or department heads.

Great leaders never ask more from their team members than they themselves are willing to do or have already done.

Team members shouldn't feel like they are doing the grunt work and that their leader is "above the minutiae." All roles are important with regard to reaching set goals and objectives and the team's leader should acknowledge that as well as be ready to get her/his hands dirty.

Wendy Thomas Williams {New York}, President and Founder
W.T. Williams Educational Consultants

TAMILYN BANNO

PURPOSE

POWDER TO THE PEOPLE:
The Heart of Production

Avid skiers dream of powder. The snow is feathery light and requires a different technique than skiing on a packed surface. Powder can get pretty deep, and some of the best runs are made when it's piled high. Balance is centered, and momentum is forward; otherwise, the skier sinks and gets stuck in the snow. There's skill in mastering the maneuver, but once it's learned, the sensation of floating down the mountain is epic.

Mastering leadership is about balance, momentum, and being centered on the people we serve. It's an engaging role, guiding individuals toward a specific goal. However, with the major concern over disengagement in the workplace, leadership is in question. There's little guidance, little trust, and little evidence of momentum.

In a conversation with Colonel Christopher Mayer, United States Army (Retired), he described to me the role of a leader. "Leadership is an art. In this case, it is the art of getting the willing obedience of others to achieve a common purpose." He says this idea is not new or original; it has been around since Xenophon and Lao Tzu. Each wrote about leadership from opposite sides of the world in the 4th century BC. (Xenophon was a Greek historian and soldier and Lao Tzu was an ancient Chinese philosopher.)

"Willing obedience is essential," Colonel Mayer concludes. "The question is how to secure that willingness, that commitment. More broadly, a leader is someone who has a vision of what can be, and the strength of will to get others to share that vision. People follow the leader because they want to—because the leader's desired end-state becomes their desire, too."

Like any art, leadership requires an innate talent, a spark that must be recognized and developed. Colonel Mayer believes many people have it, but even more do not. Like other artistic talents, there are those who go through life never knowing they have it, or who lack mentoring, or who are afraid to develop it further. Also, like the other arts, there are people that practice it who have no talent at all. "The difference is that leaders work with people rather than paint and canvas or clay. The poor leader interferes with other people achieving their own potential."

All too often, the title 'leader' is given to an individual over a department or team without a defined job description. The position can be a stepping stone or a waiting-zone until a position in a higher management level becomes available. In the case of a direct sales model, a person is a leader once he or she signs a new representative to the company. No previous leadership skills are required.

Numerous educational institutions train students to aim for the top; to be the best in the class, to become the CEO, the entrepreneur, or even the President of the United States. It's great to have high aspirations, but this mindset cultivates the unhealthy belief that if we don't reach the highest level of a company, we feel as though we failed. The truth is, not everyone is meant to be at the top. Who defines our top anyway? I truly believe the best leaders are attentive and intentional followers. Great followers become CEO's, and then they follow the direction of the company's board of directors. Joshua followed Moses for forty years before leading the Israelites into the Promised Land.

If you are a leader, you'll recognize the drive and passion to connect with others, and most importantly, to gain their trust. You can distinguish the talents of an individual, reward the accomplishments, and expect the willingness of the employee to do more, but will you? Organizations today are missing their production mark because they don't recognize the leadership deficiencies in their own management practices, but you can be the change to turn it around.

When leaders connect to people on an emotional level, trust develops and the energy of momentum begins to sizzle. According to the TINYpulse study in December 2013, "Employees in a positive mindset are generally more committed to an organization and therefore productive. This connection inspires the heart of the employees, 'If I can believe and trust my management, I'll work harder for them.'"

Inspiring leaders are pathfinders; they have a clear vision of their desires and purpose, and mentor others along the way. They are centered and focused, thinking and acting from the inside out. People don't follow leaders because of their title; they follow leaders because they share the same beliefs. Once the leader establishes a genuine relationship with their team members, moving forward with more people on board is possible.

Years ago when I was ready for a new vehicle, I visited a variety of dealerships before I made a decision. No offense to my local dealership friends, but the reason I bought a Subaru was because of the passion behind the sale. In 2008, Subaru held the #1 rating in safety above all other makers in the industry. Did I know that when I went in to look at the car? No. Did I believe the salesman? Yes. His strong conviction in the construction and safety of the car—and the safety of my children—became mine, too.

Leaders are on the right path when they believe in their purpose and the purpose of the company. Understanding *why* they do what they do is a vital first step in building team momentum. The 'why' is not about the product or even the production numbers. Numbers are the result of what happens when employees work. The 'why' is the drive and integrity of the leader.

When the leader adopts and believes whole heartedly in the vision, others will, too. If you don't know the vision or purpose statement of the company you work for, ASK! If you don't believe in its vision, it's going to be very difficult for team members to put their trust in you.

There's skill in maneuvering a team through tough terrains, but that's part of the adventure. When a leader and his or her team share the same desires and strive for the same goals, momentum strikes. And when momentum strikes, no one sinks; everyone is balanced, centered, and ready to roll.

Be Calm and Powder On!

Do you enjoy your leadership role? Pull the special details out and write them below. (Include your office décor, the training, or business travels you take.)

_____

_____

_____

_____

_____

_____

_____

_____

_____

_____

_____

Describe a terrible day at work. What events are taking place?

_____

_____

_____

_____

_____

_____

Be your best critic: How does your department or team perceive you? Are you generally happy? Are you approachable?

_____

_____

_____

_____

_____

_____

_____

_____

_____

Why do you lead? *Why do you do what you do?*

_____

_____

_____

_____

_____

_____

_____

_____

_____

_____

_____

_____

_____

TAMILYN BANNO

PART THREE

The Revelation of a Retreat

A NEW START

You gather a few of your friends around during a large social gathering and begin to tell one of the juiciest stories…EVER! You are strategic in the delivery, certain not to leave out any detail, and careful to include each suspenseful chain of events. Every piece is theatrically highlighted, from your expressive hands describing the raging thunderstorm that's rattling the double pane windows to the hush of your voice, when your eyes rendezvous with a mysterious man handing off a black attaché case in the downpour. Your friends are re-living the experience through your every syllable. If anyone were to interrupt, the story would lose all its energy. Right on cue, Kelly blares into the group and announces her arrival, "Hey, guys, what's up!"

We've all been interrupted in the middle of something, at some time, during our day—the phone call that took us off guard, the vacuum bag that exploded *(recently happened)*, or the computer that just got sick with a virus. It's annoying to have to start over, but when things aren't working out the way we believe they should, the beginning is the only productive place to start.

When I first became a leader, I was clueless as to how to lead a team. Looking back, my director wasn't the best mentor, but at that time I didn't know better, and since the company was fairly new, I'm not sure he did either. I rarely socialized or encouraged a sense of team spirit. It was a challenge for me to reach out and build relationships, and this intimidation was crippling to the team. I never realized how introverted I could be, and it was scary; probably because it was my first leadership gig, and I had zippo experience in sales. I still had an appetite to lead, but no direction or manual to follow. If I wanted to make this new venture work, I had to step out of my comfort zone and find my own way.

Starting over is what leaders should do when things aren't going as planned, especially when there's a transition in the company or when there's too many bandages covering up blunders. Allen Catherine Kagina is the Commissioner General for the Uganda Revenue Authority (URA), similar to the IRS in the U.S.. Ms. Kagina transformed the organization by first addressing the deep corruption from within the system. How? She made every person in the organization reapply for their job. She made everyone start over! Since employment is a commodity in Uganda, this changed the atmosphere in the workplace and the integrity of the employees. A new, honorable, and appreciative value system was in place.

Parents tend to be inquisitive with their children. We want to know their thoughts, inspirations, and who they want to be when they grow up. We initiate dialog that causes them to think—it's *their* start. Throughout their life we applaud their works in order to initiate motivation, and what happens? They take action. (And we love it when they take action!) We find a working pattern and with encouraging guidance, we repeat our praise. In turn, they continue to excel. The process, if you haven't figured it out, is never over. ("#EnjoyTheJourney!")

Leadership takes the same approach: *When you know what makes your team tick, encouraging words are the ultimate trick!* People, in general, desire support and encouragement. Team members and employees are people, too. I wonder if sometimes leaders bulk them into a separate sub-human category or worse, a piece of machinery, and expect something other than what they are capable of becoming.

A new start for me was to travel and train the individuals on my team in small group settings. My purpose was to visit and to let each person know how much I valued his/her work, no matter the dollar amount he/she contributed to the bottom line. I put many miles on my Subaru, getting to know as many as I could either one on one or in small groups. This was more comfortable for me, and so it became an annual summer event. This new direction inspired positive attitudes, formed friendships, and ignited a team spirit. I learned more about each person and his or her goals than I ever imagined. When we all came together for an annual conference, I was amazed with the atmosphere of warmth and good will expressed among the members. It was like a reunion of souls, yet only a few had ever physically met.

With the changes I instigated, the cog wheel began to turn and my team was connecting on new levels. The bigger picture of success was happening through smaller groups or individual sessions, beyond the monthly meetings with training, recognitions, and rewards. For years my team sales were #17 in the company. Once I began to listen and invest in the goals of my team members, we climbed to #5. Before we could even get comfortable, however, we jumped to #3; but the story gets even better.

One evening I was flipping through a few photo albums reminiscing about all the family fun we had...*on vacations*. Then it hit me...a team getaway! I would schedule a time and place where my team leaders could re-start and re-launch a new season. We could grow together while training and having fun. Yes, an off-site leadership retreat! This was the revelation; the missing link that changed the direction of *our* business.

People want to be appreciated and leaders can make that happen. Retreats are the jump start—the trigger of momentum that applauds individuals and moves them forward. After the first retreat, my team jumped to the *#1 position within 30 days*. We remained #1, month after month throughout the year and into the next, until I retired.

A retreat; it's a simple solution, right? There are many respected authors whose books and leadership models provide valuable mentoring. Leaders can and should attend conferences, webinars, and receive one-on-one coaching to fulfill their career. However, in every leadership book I've ever read, the missing chapter is the one that speaks to the value of a leadership retreat. Annual retreats are the *start*. They are the kick-off to momentum. Retreats engage, renew, and rejuvenate a team's path to success.

Don't miss it; don't miss this important piece that will change the course of your team, and the strength of your leadership.

When we shift our thinking to other people first, a shift toward momentum begins.

If you had to 'start over,' where would you begin? What would you start over, and how would you go about doing it?

_____

_____

_____

_____

_____

_____

_____

_____

_____

_____

_____

_____

Consider cleaning house. Think about your department or team, and where they really need work. Where are their struggles? What training do they need to learn or re-learn? Restart an old training program. List which ones you would start with first.

_____

_____

_____

_____

_____

_____

_____

You could organize a basic training retreat. Open your calendar and schedule a date.

Retreat Date:

_____

_____

HOW AND WHY RETREATS WORK

Most everyone remembers the fall of AIG insurance company back in 2008. Their top executives spent $440,000 at a retreat *after* the government bailed them out with billions of taxpayer's money (Sean Lengell, *The Washington Times*, October 2008). Needless to say, the public was pretty ugly about the news and sadly, corporate retreats left a sour taste in its wake. Even the more ethical retreats have taken a hiatus due to the economic recession. However, the right retreat is a proven profitable business tool and in this post-recession era, it's making a comeback.

According to the 2012 article in *Forbes Travel Guide*, "Luxury Corporate Retreats are Back," Joseph Bates, senior director of research at the Global Business Travel Association Group claims, "Travel spending went up nearly 8 percent in 2011 and is expected to continue to rise...But that doesn't necessarily mean it's back to the status quo—retreat trips are coming back smaller, shorter and with much fuller agendas than before. No one is really looking at resuming pre-recession extravagance," Bates says. "There's a balance."

Retreats are under a transformation. While some companies are returning to the grand getaway of frivolous spending, the image of quantity extravagance is consciously being replaced with the image of quality intention. Organizations are focusing on improving the individual experience in order to build trust and increase work performance.

Best-selling author and entrepreneur Jack Canfield holds annual luxury retreats, but not the ridiculously exorbitant type. His getaways are excursions with a greater inner purpose, "To become the person you need to be to achieve your goals." The elements in Mr. Canfield's retreats are comparable to the structure of MMPP. A quality retreat influences the heart of the individual in order to stir momentum.

In-service workshops are a necessary part of training. However, most likely the employees return to their desks without great stimulation or effective personal growth. Off-site retreats are favorable for stimulating creativity, connecting with team members, and ultimately generating more revenue for the organization.

"The Benefits of Holding an Off-Site Retreat" posted by *UCLA Meetings,* 2013: "On-site meetings are often much cheaper and more convenient for attendees, but do they yield the same results?" Reasons why it's a great idea for an off-site location include: *There are Fewer Distractions* resulting in more focus and less interruptions; *A New Setting* encourages more creativity and openness for new change; *Teambuilding* brings people out of their shell and helps them engage with one another; and *A Fresh Outlook* with a new perspective and energized feeling about their business is gained. Also suggested in the article was to "plan the retreat during normal working days. People are often resentful about having to use their weekends for a work retreat."

In direct sales, corporate sales, health care, or the vast of small businesses, a company's growth and stability depends upon the level of commitment from its employees. In order for current leaders to develop future leaders, it's imperative to have a clear understanding of their own goals and how they merge with those of the organization. This is the ultimate purpose of a leadership retreat. Wendy S. Goffe, a Trusts and Estates attorney in Seattle, references retreats as, "the opportunity to review a company's core values; explore its mission; and examine challenges and opportunities for the future."

The intent of a retreat is to build trust—trust between the individual and the leader. Zig Ziglar, author and motivational speaker, once said, "If people like you, they'll listen to you, but if they trust you, they'll do business with you." Trust is not guaranteed, but it's something that you can earn. It's more than just listening; your team members want to be understood. Whether or not you agree, they want you to give value to their opinion. In sales there's a golden rule: *Customers will buy from who they know and trust.* Team members are no different. They will buy into what you need them to do *when* you build a credible relationship, and not a moment before.

I recently overheard a conversation in which someone said, 'Brilliance is in communication; technology is the compliment.' This is the basis for a compelling retreat. Personal attention is given to listen to what others are saying while business training is implemented. Incorporating both at the same time invites trust and the confidence that your business will run more effectively.

An article posted in *Time Magazine,* 2012, "Do Smaller or

Larger Groups Promote Better Performance?" Jennifer Mueller, Wharton Management professor, read through research data led by Teresa Amabile, a professor at Harvard Business School, and says, "When it comes to teams less is sometimes more…On a smaller team, people knew what resources were available and felt they could ask questions." Contribution is lost in larger groups. It's easier to sit and watch…and judge. A small group retreat should be comfortable for every person. Each person's input is valuable, and every individual should know and believe that this is true.

I couldn't agree more. For a quality retreat, keep the size small. Do your best not to exceed a dozen people. If there are too many people, then it will be difficult to create the bonds necessary for building the best rapport. Splitting into groups is equally destructive; it separates team members and defeats the purpose of creating synergy.

Retreats can be anywhere, even in a basement or back yard. Take time to research destinations. We are surrounded by a world of majestic beauty. We all yearn for more; to belong more, to love more, to breathe deeper, and to receive gifts that take our breath away. What natural beauty brings appreciation and peace to your mind? Where were you the last time you marveled at God's creation? There are countless places available for retreats, and with the internet at our hands, imagination can become a reality.

In the fascinating article "Are You Getting Enough Vitamin N? The Surprising Health Benefits of Nature" (*Women's Health Magazine*, 2013), leading naturalist Richard Louv, author of *The Nature Principle*, says: "We can be happier, healthier, and smarter if we weave more nature into our lives." He points to a surge in studies that strongly suggest a link between the outside and the inside, and that the best mind-body medicine may lay right beyond your front door.

Sunsets and sunrises speak to us. When researching locations, find a place where time stands still, or where you can stand still and forget about time. I had access to an incredibly beautiful beach front property for my first leadership retreat. Angela, one of my team leaders, walked through the front door and, with only a peep "hello," headed straight to the balcony's ocean view. I watched out the window as she consciously breathed in the salty air and smiled over the roaring waves. A few moments later I joined her, and the only spoken word was the tear of gratitude that fell upon her face.

Settling team members when they first arrive can be challenging. Restlessness is common in the beginning, especially for first time attendees. Do not rush to break their barriers. This is their retreat and they will soon let go, but from my experience, the grace of nature plays a large role in penetrating some of the toughest shells.

Retreats are events that leaders dream for; they are gifts where authenticity is captured. Find a place that *woos* you. Take time to travel and explore hidden healing treasures. A retreat flies by and nature gives us the resources we need to begin an inward reflection.

Retreats heal. Souls are stirred. Humbling occurs. Walls crumble. Strength re-builds. Collaboration ignites. Productions soar!

Could you use a little healing, soul stirring, walls crumbling, and productions soaring?

Where is your woo-place?

_____

_____

_____

_____

_____

_____

_____

_____

_____

_____

If you were on a small vacation with friends, list some
activities you would be doing.

_____

_____

_____

_____

_____

_____

_____

_____

_____

_____

_____

_____

_____

TAMILYN BANNO

72

LOCK N' LOAD, BABY!:
The Momentum Model of Leadership Development

My all-time favorite retreats are when leaders get together with other leaders. The amount of energy pulled from the room is invigorating and empowering. Leaders absorb this audacious intensity; they are brilliantly influenced and ready for action. Lock n' load, baby—momentum is about to explode!

Momentum begins with a power play; it starts when a driving force is initiated by a stimulus. In this case, the stimulus is the influence of the leader. The measure of the influence will determine the strength and speed of the momentum.

In sports one great play can throw a team into momentum. One kick, one catch or one ace can change the course of a game. In football, the quarterback's purpose is to direct his team toward the goal. The team trusts him to initiate a power play, and that his skill will have an influence on the final outcome. In business, the leader is like the quarterback; his or her purpose is to direct the team toward the goal, and one play can influence the momentum of the whole team.

Momentum is an effortless flow of energy. If there is little energy to begin with, there will be little to no influence, and therefore, little team movement. If there is a lot of energy, there will be greater influence resulting in a positive and powerful movement.

In what ways are you energizing your team? Your influence is the measurable energy which sparks them into motion. Is your influence strong enough, or is it too strong? Is it positive or negative? More importantly, is it authentic? What feedback are you observing from your team, and are you proactive in making adjustments to the quality of your leadership?

Influence inspires people to act and behave in a specific manner. What if leaders promoted a positive influence over their team? What if they got into the game and initiated a play? What if they mentored and spread encouragement? Imagine the momentum! Imagine the production!

As stated earlier, when you know your purpose and direction, others will follow; when they believe that you have their best interest at heart, they will work harder for you. Just like the quarterback, when the leader's goals are clearly aligned with the team, the power of momentum is locked in place. The leader is loaded with confidence and prepared to move the team toward the ultimate win. Once momentum begins to flow, the next step is to nurture and direct its course down the field.

How do you sustain momentum and connect with the team to keep them moving? Simple. Through acts of motivation: incentives, recognitions, rewards, and promotions. Motivation is much like dangling carrots in front of a horse;

enticing people with rewards encourages them to reach a certain goal. However, motivation is successful only when it *follows* an energizing and stimulating influence: the momentum of the leader. A leader who attempts to lead without first having a genuine interest in the individuals on the team will run out of carrots long before motivating them into action. I've been there. You've been there. We've tried every trick in the book to motivate our team and often come short to throwing in the towel. The truth is people don't want carrots; they don't even like carrots. They want chocolate. *They want us*, and we're the Willy Wonka of the chocolate factory.

People want leaders who get involved. They trust leaders who can physically and mentally relate to their jobs and their challenges. When the influence is authentic, positive, and full of energy, it's enticingly sweet. Plain and simple: Momentum lasts longer and motivation is more effective when people know, trust, and like you, first.

When leaders stimulate momentum, teams become motivated, and businesses flourish!

A visionary leader will be able to see the momentum in motion so he or she can direct and balance the flow. With a bird's eye view, the leader can assess the energy and prepare for any bends or struggles in the road. A leader can strategically maneuver people around, see where communication is lacking, increase training, and provide recognition. In other words, a leader can see *when, where, and who* to encourage in order to reach the desired destination.

A visionary leader is much like a conductor of an orchestra.

He knows the music and how each instrument fits into the master piece. The conductor understands the composition and directs each section. He knows when the strings should descend and when the percussions should ascend. He can make everybody play, or only a few at a time. His influence controls the momentum. He's the maestro, *the leader.*

People need leaders, and they follow the ones who get involved and inspire them with purpose, direction and trust. When we put ourselves into the game, it's a powerful play.

Leaders, your influence is the heart and soul of The Momentum Model. How you play, when you play, and *if you play,* will determine the success of your team. The science behind the Momentum Model prepares leaders for an enlightened leadership mission.

Lock n' load, baby! Your team is on fire!

PART FOUR

The MMPP
Leadership Retreat

DEEPER INTO THE ELEMENTS

When facilitating a retreat, it's important to provide a plan that holds unique value which can ultimately have a positive effect on everyone's business. Throughout years of dinner parties and fundraisers, I found that attaching a theme to an event adds a third dimension and sweetens the adventure. Since appreciation and training were my motives, the first retreat I held circled around gratitude and team productivity. The format of Maintenance, Motivation, Purpose, and Plan (MMPP) whispered into my heart and became the foundation for the first, and all future, retreats. Weaving a theme into these elements set this retreat apart from others I've ever attended.

As mentioned earlier, leaders require *Maintenance,* especially after working a very busy season. The significance of a quiet withdrawal from the tenacity of work is healing. The focus of *Maintenance* is to immediately melt the mind and body into a serene state. This healing element is all about lowering the outer shield, letting go of the materialistic world in order to open and accept a deep sense of worthiness and appreciation. *Maintenance* leaves us vulnerable, yet secure.

The next element is *Motivation,* training and empowering skills with a lighthearted twist. As a leader it's important to be able to discuss challenges with team members and to ignite a spark back into the work and home. Everyone desires a motivational spirit. It's engaging and adventurous! *Motivation* is the easiest element to lose, and sometimes it's the hardest to get back. Daily *motivation* is inspired by leaders; without it, there is no passion to move forward.

The element of *Purpose* brings us back to our roots. There are brain storming activities and personal vision exercises that clarify a more focused path. Here, fears are released and an inner drive is reclaimed. *Purpose* is empowering. It gives rise to our joy, strengthens our trust, and renews our personal and company's vision.

Never leave a retreat without a *Plan*. The time away offers great reflection and builds a warm community, but not knowing what to do following the retreat can be devastating. Implementing the next steps gives concrete direction and a sense of security. While *Purpose* may plant the seed, *Plan* enables it to grow!

One More Detail: The Secret Ingredient

The Element of Surprise

There's something about spontaneity that makes me giggle. I am a huge fan of taking something to the next level in order to blow someone's mind. It's my favorite game to play. Every year was a challenge to bring something bigger and better (not necessarily in monetary terms) to our six children on Christmas morning. I'm not sure if this is considered a selfish act of kindness, but I'd do just about anything to see that 'wow' on their faces. Eyes are all-telling and when I see them come to life, my heart sings.

We all enjoy an unexpected ingredient that sweeps us off our feet. An impulsive addition gives permission for team members to feel the whimsical wonder of youth. Surprising leaders, however, can sometimes backfire. Leaders tend to be control freaks, and someone can get hurt if you take away his/her joystick.

Surprises have to be subtle and safe for everyone. After all, you're creating a surrender situation. A surprise, whether good or bad, can sometimes be taken as an attack. Without it, however, there's no souvenir for them to bring home, there's nothing to write home about, and there's nothing that will bring them back to another retreat.

In one of my evening retreat training sessions, I gave the team an autographed copy of a leadership book and asked them to read over a specific chapter. This was a little light homework in preparation for a round table discussion we would be having the following day. During our lunch break, as a little surprise, I arranged for the author to join us, you know, just to see their jaws drop. (Mission accomplished!)

Leaders, in planning your agenda, never give out all the details. Always leave a subtle air of surprise.

Maintenance, Motivation, Purpose, and Plan are the four key elements to increasing personal growth while building a high performance team. Other leadership development courses are available; however, I find that this particular retreat has the most powerful and residual impact.

List some themes you could use for your retreat. Is there a new product line coming out you could bounce off of—or new training material you could stretch into a fun topic? Don't limit yourself; think outside the box. Definitely ask friends and family who are not with the company for ideas. And ask children; they can be very imaginative!

_____

_____

_____

_____

_____

_____

_____

_____

_____

_____

What surprises would you bring to the retreat?

_____

_____

_____

_____

_____

_____

_____

_____

_____

_____

TAMILYN BANNO

Traveling through the Elements of

Maintenance, Motivation, Purpose, and Plan

In a business like this it's important to understand the difference between training and coaching. Examples of training could be: sharing product knowledge, teaching someone about the computer system, and showing examples of how to create a host or sponsoring packet. And while there will always be reasons for ongoing training, there is a finite aspect to training—a beginning and an end.

Coaching, on the other hand, is ongoing. Coaching involves helping people strategize and take action. Coaching helps people stay on track with their goals through accountability and reality checks. When you're in business for yourself, it's the coaching that keeps consultants from feeling they are all by themselves.

But one of the key reasons that consultants will succeed with a company is beyond skills learned and the accountability. It's the connections made, and the sense of community that builds lifelong friendships and loyalty to the team and the business. Successful leaders typically build those connections through monthly team meetings. Like-minded consultants start to hear each other's stories, cheer each other on to success, help each other overcome challenges, all while working toward a common goal. Leaders can enhance these bonds by including activities outside the business. Volunteering for a worthy cause, holding a family picnic, or even Christmas caroling together create memories and connections.

Incentives are a standard part of the direct selling business model. And while companies often offer a variety of large and small incentives, successful leaders can do that too. Prizes for an incentive should be varied, but keep in mind that we should strive to create a 'moment'—it's not just about the 'memento.' Recognition in public, in front of peers, or even family members, gives a consultant the opportunity to feel proud of his/her accomplishment. As Mary Kay Ash said, "We all wear a sign that says 'Make Me Feel Important.'" You'll find your team will work hard just to earn lunch with you, the leader. It's not about the 'presents;' it's about providing your 'presence' that will make a difference.

The ultimate way to create that time with you and the team is to offer a team retreat. Share your home or rent a location for the group to spend a couple of days. It doesn't have to be expensive. In fact, some of the best retreats I've held and attended were the ones that resembled a high school slumber party. People on couches, bunked up, without pretenses (and often without makeup)—that's where our walls come down and true bonds are formed.

The format for Tami's retreat (Maintenance, Motivation, Purpose and Plan) created the ideal structure to accomplish an unforgettable, motivational retreat. The Maintenance segment offered a form of recognition as consultants were pampered. So few women make the time to take care of themselves and this segment not only offered pampering, but enlightened many to the importance of taking care of themselves to be the best they can be.

The Motivation segment offered insight into 'what CAN be.' Training on the 'how to' be successful in the business re-inspired participants. When people have a clear sense of expectations, as well as impact of their actions, they are successful. The problem is, we often lose sight of those expectations and impact because we're pulled in so many directions.

We keyed into the 'why we do what we do' in the Purpose segment. How our actions affect us, our team, our family, our leader, etc. Again, it's easy to lose sight of the 'what' and the 'why' because we get caught up in our own whirlwind day to day.

And with any good meeting, a clear call to action sends the team off with direction. By wrapping up with the Plan segment, goals and action steps were defined in writing and shared out loud to the team. This was very powerful. As everyone got back to reality, they felt compelled to keep their promises to the team and the leader that made this amazing experience possible.

The Maintenance, Motivation, Purpose, and Plan format can be adapted for any business and any size team. It works for a weekend retreat, but could also be used as a structure for a conference, or even on a small scale for a 2-hour monthly meeting.

Marianne Friedlund, Director of Training, Ava Anderson Non Toxic, Retreat Attendee

MAINTENANCE

Goal: Reduce stress and gain a peaceful balance.

Solitude is a precious commodity. When we take time to rejuvenate our body, mind, and spirit, a peaceful work and life balance nestles in our soul. We can take better care of others and inspire creativity when we refresh ourselves.

The Law of Receptivity
The key to effective giving is to stay open to receiving.

The Go-Giver

Personal Reflection

MY MESS IS MY MESSAGE

"This is the age of storytellers. We live in a dream society and those who capture the attention and hearts of their audience have immense power to lead and influence." —Bo Eason

I couldn't stop shivering. It was late November; I was sitting in my car staring out the window for some time before turning on the engine. I paused to notice how dark and still the world is at 4 am. All I could hear was the thought in my head; 'Are you really doing this?'

Everyone has a story of brokenness, including myself. However, leaving at this time was more than an attempt to deal with emotional struggles. There was another force fearlessly drawing me *toward* something.

I entered the address in the GPS on the dashboard: 1,061 miles to my destination. The only company I had was a book on tape and a box of Kleenex, yet I was oddly prepared for this road trip. I had detached from emotions as I packed boxes, organized bills, and caught up with laundry. For the first time, Christmas presents were wrapped a month early, waiting for the Great day. My departure during the holidays may have been lousy, especially for my six children, but I couldn't explain the strength in knowing I was doing the right thing.

Seventeen hours later I arrived. I walked into the kitchen and felt a chill of loneliness fill my bones. I noticed a devotional book sitting on the counter and opened it to the daily message. Slowly I whispered the scripture written, 'Leave everything behind and follow me'—and then it hit me. *He* brought me here. *He* orchestrated it all in order to get my attention. My knees buckled; I gasped and grabbed the counter, catching myself from falling. I stared out the window and wept in disbelief. *It's the holidays! I just left everything and everybody behind! What was I thinking?* My heart broke into pieces and in a desperate plea I cried out, "God! Please have a really good reason!"

Life is hard. It's hard when we feel a loss of control and everything is crumbling around us. It's hard when we devote so much time to something or someone we love, but the return of investment doesn't measure up. It's hard—no, horrible—when we put our heart on the line, but fall into the trap of feeling unworthy.

Does our happiness depend on the love we receive? Is our fulfillment measured by the respect we acquire? That's how this game of life works, right? Isn't it someone else's job to reciprocate and complete us? Our spouse, our family, our work?

Pain is universal. Some people carry it in their hearts, other people carry it in their steps, or in their speech, maybe it's in their bank accounts, or something that interrupts their dreams. Pain touches all of us; it's a part of our story—our purpose—and it connects us to each other.

Leadership is built upon a message, a story—*your story*. It's opening yourself up so others can see your authenticity, your embarrassing moments, your shameful moments, your spills and falls; people want to relate to you and they want to do so *not* through your successes, but through your pains and your mistakes.

People connect with weaknesses. When you begin to tell a story their eyes lock-in; you've got their attention. As you tell your tale of triumph, they lean in; as their leader, they want to know how you came out on the other side. Be very careful; there is a balance so use discretion. You are developing a story of conquer, not a set-up or stage for sympathy. Leaders do not live or relive the past; they are examples of how to move forward.

By sharing a part of yourself you become 'tangible' and people start to believe in you; you're 'one of them' and trust begins to develop. You are magically magnetic and can influence and lead through the mess of your message.

Vulnerability is the new power in leadership.

"The single most important skill you must have to lead is: The ability to tell your own story" (Bo Eason: A Personal Story Power, www.jeremeyhutchens.com). "Same is true for you. You may be a leader who's not leading because people don't know how to latch onto you and follow. Your personal story is the connective tissue between you and your potential clients. Today's success is built on relationship, authenticity, and deep personal connection."

When people see a piece of themselves in a leader, a connection is made and trust is captured. This is the exciting foundation momentum is built upon. Sometimes, however, we choose to be authentic in some areas of our life, but not in every area. We tend to sweep stuff under the rug, and this interferes with the flow of momentum. Energy is sucked out of our stream. There's a gaping hole that we thought really wouldn't have an effect on our success, but we were wrong.

I was wrong.

Distractions in my relationships took a life of their own. I never realized my personal problems were affecting the success of my business, but that's exactly what was happening. Momentum started to drag and I felt the resistance. It was like running a race with lead shoes on my feet. I kept running and running as fast as I could, but could never reach full speed. The problem became obvious, I wasn't 'all-in;' I chose which parts in life I wanted to be authentic and which parts I'd worry about later. Well, later arrived. God must've said, 'Enough; it's time to go.' So I got in my car, at 4 am…

As leaders, our influence needs to be authentic and powerful and based on our own tales. Retreats are where stories are strengthened. They are where we learn more about ourselves and how to impact more people. They are short, personal breaks to a place of peace where our walls come down and we shift from chaos to clarity.

Everyone requires a little *maintenance*. Interestingly enough, most of us wait until a near crash experience to allow ourselves the time for rejuvenation. When we don't give ourselves the permission to 'check-out' for a weekend, our body will tell us—or He will.

Once and awhile we need to loosen our grip from this world,

press the pause button, and absorb life's gifts. A retreat cleanses the spirit and balances flow so connections and trust can build.

FIRST NOTE TO SELF: My story is my strength

Maintenance is priceless.

Taking time for oneself is often perceived as selfish, but in reality it is selfless. Without making time for reflection, maintenance, and reaffirming our purpose we lose our self and the joy we find in life.

Kathy Burke (Illinois), Independent Educational Consultant, Retreat Attendee

"DANGER, DANGER!"

There are agencies that provide companies comprehensive strategies for maintenance management programs. They analyze current work tracking and development, and then suggest alternative resources for better efficiency. The goal of these agencies is to improve the level of service, growth, and longevity of the companies by taking preventative measures.

Preventive maintenance invites longevity of a product or service, but unfortunately it's highly neglected. Being proactive in business, home, and health alleviates *responsive* maintenance where correcting and repairing the unexpected takes precedence. A maintenance program left on its own is often found fighting fires. Being prepared, like the motto of a good Boy Scout, will allow you to plan ahead, with foresight, so not every surprise is devastating.

Preventive maintenance offers a hardy growth for any organization. One step ahead of an outcome is being responsible and even protective. You wouldn't wander out in subzero degree weather without wearing a jacket for fear of freezing. You wouldn't run a marathon without years of training first for fear of collapsing on the trail. Being proactive means you will mow your lawn twice a week so the grass will not grow too thick to cut. You will change the oil in your car when it's required so your engine will not break down. *(Been there, done that; major oops!)* Preventive maintenance is a big, big deal and yet, many of us try to get by without it in every facet of life. Why? Because it takes time, and time is a valuable commodity. Why isn't our well-being a valuable commodity?

No matter how prepared we think we may be, inevitably, some part of our life will break down. Hopefully, it will take us into a better and stronger place, but in the meantime, it can wear on us, break us apart, and tear us into pieces. Being prepared helps us to recover with less emotional damage and with more confidence of a better tomorrow.

What if we practiced a proactive life? What if leaders were proactive? With the taxing stress that comes along with the leadership role, what if we respected ourselves enough to take preventative measures? What if we thought more of ourselves, and our business, to take a break and map out a healthy plan? We have the power to strengthen our physical and mental health, and the health of our leadership, but we rarely take the opportunity.

Sometimes we won't take personal time-outs, getaways, massages, or meditation classes because they're considered frivolous spending. A few acquaintances of mine even feel embarrassed if friends or neighbors see them entering a day spa for fear they'll be labeled pompous and spoiled. Regardless, not every self-giving gift needs to have a price tag. Getaways could be a quiet walk in nature, and meditations are often in solitude. God gave us a body, mind, and spirit; surely He is expecting us to take care of all three. Preventive maintenance is what He hopes we will do to strengthen our inner peace so we can increase our longevity and welcome more abundance into our lives.

When we maintain proper care for ourselves, we are equipped to take care of others. When we are better prepared, we are more patient and make better parents, better friends, and better leaders.

The ability to build and maintain a healthy relationship with an employee heightens the trust and respect between the individual and the leader. Handwritten notes, coffee gift cards, treats left at his or her desk, are all gestures of appreciation. Recognizing birthdays, anniversaries, or random tokens given for no reason builds a stronger connection. Personal phone calls to an individual team member can make him or her feel more visible, and more important. All of these suggestions can be done at the leadership level, regardless of whether or not it's written in the company's training manual.

In the ten years Douglas Conant was CEO of the Campbell Soup Company he wrote out 30,000 handwritten thank-you notes to his employees. "I made it personal at Campbell." Conant was determined to create and maintain a high-level of engagement and succeeded with his exceptional touch *(www.forbes.com/business/)*.

Human beings are naturally social people. We enjoy, even crave, being together. According to the Gallup Organization, people who have one or more good friends at work tend to be happier employees. As leaders, we can encourage and help maintain healthy relationships through social activities and community projects.

As leaders, we should continue to build and maintain good

relationships by reaching throughout our various organizations. It's a great way to collaborate with other department leaders, and it sets an example to other employees. Invite a colleague to lunch. Little interactions go a long way. Maintain your social media status; reply to people's postings on Facebook, Twitter, and LinkedIn.

Although we may not be able to keep everyone happy, it's worth the effort. When things do go wrong and we're faced with disgruntled employees, disturbances can be kept to a minimum.

Schedule personal time for meditation, nature walks, yoga, or other spa services. Cultivate a good rapport with your team, but remember to restore your own balance. Ultimately, maintenance is for healing so new growth can happen.

List what preventative maintenance measures you do for yourself. Do you often take walks to relieve stress? Exercise and eat right to maintain a healthy body? Yoga? Stretching classes? Bike riding? Take special time outs for reading? Meditation? Pedicures? Massage?

How do you serve yourself so you are physically and mentally able to serve others?

_____

_____

_____

_____

_____

_____

Write down the birthdays of everyone in your department or team.

Send annual birthday cards beginning this month.

Team Roster/Birthdays:

My first retreat was 8 years ago when I first started in the direct sales business. I remember it well and can still feel the overwhelming sense of pride today as I opened that invitation. It was to an overnight retreat that only the top producers were invited to attend and I was one of them!

That retreat and the many more that I have attended and/or hosted myself have shaped me into the person I am today and I am forever thankful.

Retreats offer everyone who attends the chance to dig deep, unearth their roots and discover the WHY of their personal journey. When we make time to be with other like-minded leaders who will support us, we allow ourselves to DREAM BIG and break down the barriers that keep us from believing we can accomplish anything.

At retreats we learn, share, grow and find our authentic and abundant purpose. My DREAM BIG wish for you is simple. If you have never allowed yourself time away at a retreat before, this will open your heart to saying "Yes" at the next invitation. We all have a gift to share with others, we just need to unwrap it!

Lisa J. Buben (Florida), Rodan and Fields Executive Consultant

THE INFLUENCE OF LEADERSHIP

"The day soldiers stop bringing you their problems is the day you have stopped leading them." –Colin Powell

The day you realize your team members haven't been contacting you with their struggles is the defining moment you need to step up your game! Chances are you're the one who failed to communicate and more importantly, failed to listen.

Hey, I get it, not everyone is going to be happy or interconnect with each other, and that's okay, but there's still a great need for leaders who *lead*. Influencing individuals is the key to a successful business, but it's difficult when the majority of workers hate their jobs.

If only 13% of employees are actively engaged, then how does that reflect on the role of the leader? Employees want to feel they are contributing to the bigger picture; they are hungry to contribute and to be motivated. They want to make a difference, and they look to their team leaders for that inspiration. That's you! Have you been up to the challenge? If not, you're not alone.

With the 2007 downturn in the economy, the stock market,

housing market, and job market all resulted in evictions, foreclosures, and the closing of businesses. Were you on your knees praying? I was! Every person I know hunkered down; we entertained less, spent less, and smiled less. In 2007, we became leader-less.

Leaders were emotionally burned. Their role toppled over when the inspiration to lead left. Many lost their titles and even their jobs. Today, people are still jobless and live in debt, but I see an emotional strength on the rise. Small businesses are coming back to life and banks are beginning to lend money again, but sadly there's a stale conversation hanging around the water coolers; leadership is dead.

Motivation plays the essential key in employee engagement, but leaders are timid, afraid to take risks, and some are clueless as to how to engage teams. With the help of behavioral economics, however, leaders might be able to gain more insight.

> *"One of the most important discoveries of behavioral economics is how little our behavior is influenced by our intentions, and how much it is influenced by context." –Zoe Chance, Yale University*

Behavioral economics offers a better understanding of the different attitudes and conducts on the emotional levels in order to increase engagement. It's a personal approach to training and coaching which can lead to profitability for both the individual and the company.

Getting people to make valuable choices becomes easier when they are influenced by actions, specifically, positive reinforcement. In many organizations, a compliment or acknowledging an achievement is an effort, uncomfortable, and even sometimes considered taboo. However, being consistent with rewarding accomplishments and achievements is what makes the difference between a lack of production and an increase in performance.

Where is the heart of your leadership? What qualities are you nurturing within your team? They may be working in the field, representing the company with an attitude *reflecting your leadership skills*. Are they confident? Are customers happy? Is your team engaged? What feedback are you receiving? Are you listening?

When Howard Schultz purchased the Starbucks chain, he revamped the entire organization. His vision included more variety of coffee beverages with colorful names; Macchiato, Caramel Mocha Frappuccino, and Chai Tea Latte, just to name a few. He also created a friendly atmosphere where customers could hang out and enjoy their coffee. The most profound change, however, was his improvement with the company-employee relationship.

Schultz was convinced that a welcoming and energetic spirit would increase sales. He decided to initiate a training program with the intent to educate and prepare employees who would enjoy serving customers. "Service is a lost art in America. It's not viewed as a professional job to work behind a counter," Schultz says. "We don't believe that. We want to provide our people with dignity and self-esteem, so we offer tangible benefits" (Entrepreneur, October 2008). Schultz believes if his team is happy, his customers will be, too.

When the habits of leaders become centered on the values and respect of their team, a domino effect transpires, electrifying customers in its path. The relationship you establish *is* the motivating difference between lack and increase. Momentum is based on your lead and determined by the art of your interpersonal skills. Some leaders believe they can step in and motivate a department without first connecting and listening in a meaningful way. It might work once or twice while they try to figure you out, but ultimately, it won't last.

What energy are you influencing upon them and are you using incentives to help motivate them to reach their goals? What is driving your team to move and work harder for you?

Motivation is what you provide to continue movement. It is the piece or factor, that keeps momentum flowing. In order to *maintain* momentum you can introduce motivational incentives or 'small wins' to reach the bigger goal. When you keep connecting with your team, they will be inspired. If (and when) you lose sight of one or more along the way, don't be afraid, just rally.

Retreats capture visions and prepare teams for action. As a leader, continue to communicate and connect with your team so that when your retreat happens, momentum can fire.

Does your team know and trust you? Make a list of the people under your supervision. Put a check mark next to the ones you communicate with regularly and write why you believe they trust you.

Not sure you're building trusting relationships? Begin this week by showing your gratitude. Leave random notes on desks, pick up the phone, or strike up friendly conversations with encouraging words. Revisit this list monthly and try to maintain healthy communication with every person on your team.

DEEPER STILLL: The Great Influencer

Inevitably, at one time or another, something drastic or even damaging will happen to our business and/or our personal lives. We will become overwhelmed and desperate for help. If we're not deeply grounded in faith, then we will turn to something or someone else—trusting the golden calf or false gods—to make things right. It is our choice to put our faith into whom or what we believe. Whomever we designate as our 'go-to,' however, will have a major effect on our decisions and attitudes in our work and home life.

We are promised to have an authentic purpose in life, but when doubt and direction cloud our mind, self-worth can get thrown out the window. We begin to measure acts of kindness and lose our faith in love. If we are 'uniquely knitted together,' then who holds the knitting needles of influence? Why do we get so unraveled, and how do we stitch ourselves back together in order to reclaim our purpose?

The personal "mess" in my story that I shared at the beginning of this segment was during a difficult time when I began to question my path, my marriage, and my faith. To add to the mayhem, I had lost both parents and my six siblings were spread all over the states struggling to find kinship. My own children were grown and either leaving for college or moving out of state, and those who I thought were close friends, were not. There was emotional feeling of betrayal and abandonment stirring in my heart, so I pooled any sense of self-worth and contentment from my husband, which was fruitless. I worked so hard to receive love and assurance, but it only came in weak doses. The more I tried, the more sullen my mood, and the lonelier I became.

I poured more hours into my job, trying to fill the void; it worked for a while, but the problem remained. I was scared and didn't feel I was good enough for just about anything or anybody. There were days the label of inadequacy was superglued to my soul; my laughter left, my confidence took a hike, and my gut felt like a black hole. I needed space, time to think, and a place to heal my hurting heart.

The time away was spent reading, praying, attending meditation classes, and walking in nature. Serenity was what I hoped to achieve, yet so much more was restored. I came to understand a deeper level of behavior and how it was altered by influence. The emotions I had been displaying were the result of whom I had allowed to affect my behavior. It was my choice to respond the way I did, and every outcome was affected by that decision. *But who was it? Who was I allowing to influence me?*

An authentic lifestyle should naturally flow from our faith, family, and work. Sometimes, the flow is blocked and personalities become tainted. I admit that for a long time I depended on my husband to complete my happiness. The Bible says to acknowledge and trust in the Lord, and He will make our paths straight. We must lean on Him and not on man. I was leaning the wrong way.

Being honest and genuine should be the character we exhibit, all the time. Yet every day we allow other people to dictate our feelings and rule our emotions. As hard as we try not to let their comments or attitudes affect our behavior, it happens to most of us, every day. And every time we try to stop the infiltration, we realize we're simply not strong enough.

What if we chose the authenticity of God's Love to influence our behavior? What if we consciously invited Him to every occasion, in everything we do, at home and at the office? What if we ascribed to His aid before making decisions or taking on the troubles of this world? What if we forgave more and allowed Him to make the final judgment?

We all make choices, some are good and some are not so good. Every decision we make will influence a trail of other people. What we hear on the television, what we read on Facebook or Twitter, what we do and say at the office or at home, all infiltrate into our daily lives and impact more people than we realize.

Take the example of disciplining a child over breakfast: You have to punish your son for a valid reason. Most often, this decision will produce a lousy mood so, in turn, he lashes out at his younger brother, and then that brother becomes upset so he calls his little sister an awful name and she sobs and sobs her way to school. And that's just the *beginning* of a bad day.

Consider a fling at the office: Your manager is having an extramarital affair with an employee. People at work find out so naturally, gossip hits every water cooler and happy hour in town. Besides the open wounds that will never really heal at home, they each have a wrecked reputation and have lost respect and *trust* with other co-workers. Their choice results in an irreversible and surmountable trickle affect, and their actions will probably last for the remainder of his or her career. A manager or leader who justifies a poor choice has a very difficult road ahead.

The decisions you make will profoundly influence many people. As a leader, you are faced with tough confrontations, every day. You have to put out more fires than Smokey the Bear. Without a guide, you are left to depend on your own wisdom and, inevitably, you will fumble. This is why communication is important between you and God. He will help you make the right choices if you invite the conversation. And when trials are overwhelming and poor choices are made, He is the One holding the knitting needles that can mend you back together.

When I tried to live and work independently from Him, I was never, ever satisfied. I thought I was supposed to be the super-hero, strong enough to manage love on my own and to take care of my family. God surely made me one tough-cookie, but He never intended for me to go through life without Him. Couldn't someone have clued me in on this revelation earlier? Maybe someone did, and I just wasn't listening. Momentum was restored because of the retreat— because He came to tell me to *lean on Him*, and this time, I was listening.

We live a full life when we acknowledge and trust in our Great Influencer. We can only be who we were truly meant to be when we live in harmony with Him. I truly believe that, as leaders, *we are able to lead others to their innate potential when our thoughts and actions align with His.* He is our God who created our purpose.

Life is hard. Leadership is hard. We need time to let go of all the attitudes, behaviors, and guilt that are building walls around our hearts so we can restore our true self, our true purpose, and direction.

Reading helps, prayer helps, meditation helps, nature helps; retreats help.

The ability to work from a loving and serving heart changed the way I interacted with people and the way they interacted with me. My leadership was in full bloom, and still is today. So are my path, my marriage, and my faith.

Who influences your behavior?

_____

_____

Is there someone blocking the flow of your momentum; a
relationship or co-worker? List those you are struggling with
and how you can restore peaceful energy.

_____

_____

_____

_____

_____

_____

_____

_____

Do you believe your leadership is based on authenticity? Are you the same person at home as you are at work? Explain.

_____

_____

_____

_____

_____

_____

_____

_____

_____

_____

_____

_____

_____

_____

_____

_____

_____

Are you searching for deeper fulfillment? In what areas? Explain.

_____

_____

_____

_____

_____

_____

_____

_____

_____

_____

_____

_____

_____

_____

_____

THE HUMBLE LEADER

Humility is often presumed to be a weakness, when actually it's an enormous asset to your leadership. Humility is being real, approachable, and honest with yourself and with those you lead. Max Lucado, best-selling author, says it best; "True humility is not thinking lowly of yourself, but thinking accurately of yourself."

In my effort to gain a broader understanding of how leaders today interact with new hires and new graduates, I interviewed a number of young adults (Gen Y) about their experiences when they were applying for jobs. In one particular group, the new graduates related to me that the interview process itself was sometimes daunting; three to five phone conversations took place before being considered to sit with the final hiring agent.

The hiring agents were leaders from HR departments, upper management, and sometimes CEO's. Sadly, the arrogance arising from the dialog, despite the industry, was a typical encounter. Disengaged mannerisms, wandering eyes, and smug sarcasm were the most common remarks these young people experienced. Most of these applicants left the interviews feeling vulnerable and sometimes guilty, believing that somehow they were an imposition. One of them commented, "If the person knows before I go into the final interview that the position has been filled or that I'm not the right fit, at least act interested. It's so demeaning."

I wonder if leaders, whether hiring or not, realize the image they leave in their wake. Is it really necessary to depreciate someone who is eager to learn or work for the company? I understand it's a competitive world and companies have to sift through a lot of rubble, but shouldn't there be an appropriate use of power and etiquette? It sets the first tone of leadership to impressionable graduates.

Jim Collins, author of the best seller book, *Good to Great; Why Some Companies Make the Leap and Others Don't*, launched a research project identifying elite companies that made the leap from having good-to-great results. In comparison, the research team studied similar companies that failed to make the leap. The findings included an unusual leadership trait consistent with the good-to-great companies. "Compared to high-profile leaders with big personalities who make headlines and become celebrities, the good-to-great leaders seem to have come from Mars. Self-effacing, quiet, reserved, even shy—these leaders are a paradoxical blend of personal humility and professional will."

The leader working in an organization which recognizes that he or she is not perfect allows team members to accept the fact that mistakes are inevitable, and happen to everyone. Leadership is about taking risks; it's about using the broken pieces in order to build something or someone better. Humility is a spirit that identifies with humanity; it's the ability to welcome weaknesses gracefully.

A brazen personality can be difficult to handle in any

department or team. The attitude from one person can stifle an entire group from cinching a new client or being promoting to a new level. At one time or another, we've probably all shared in the guilt of being presumptuous, talking about others, or making swift judgments. Listening to another point of view is admirable; taking a moment to *understand* another point of view shows respect.

After my high school graduation, I went on vacation with my cousin and a few of her friends. I didn't know the other girls coming along, but it didn't matter. During those years I was fearlessly social.

One day we rented mopeds, six of us on three scooters. We took off, laughing side by side with no direction in mind. Being a natural leader, I accelerated to the front of the pack and led them around town, swerving in and out of rural streets. After a while we stopped and someone asked, "Where to now?" I said, "This way!" Immediately following was a sneering remark, "Do you think you're the only one who has an opinion?"

My jaw dropped. I was so busy doing what I wanted to do that I was careless not to ask anyone else. My intentions were never to cause resentment; in hindsight, however, I should have invited more input. My opinion matters, but it's not the only one in the room. She was right, and from that one incident years ago, I'm a better leader today.

The Law of Influence from the book *The Go-Giver* states: "Your influence is determined by how abundantly you place other peoples' interests first." This does not mean to allow oneself to be taken advantage of or that one should never take risks. What I do believe is that inside every person is a piece of Divinity. God doesn't love me any more than He loves my neighbor…or another leader. The point is to remember that we are all valued at a high price, and that value should be respected by every person. When you believe the success of the team is as important, and sometimes more than your own, you become a humble leader. Retreats give you the collective time to realize what you're actually achieving.

Humility by itself does not make a great leader; humility is a characteristic great leaders embrace and develop. It's a life skill to learn, often through a personal experience. When humility slaps you in the face, don't hit back. This is the growth spirt where arrogance and grace collide. It's a gift. Open it and keep it close.

"The challenge of leadership is to be strong, but not rude; be kind, but not weak; be bold, but not bully; be thoughtful, but not lazy; be humble, but not timid; be proud, but not arrogant; have humor, but without folly." —Jim Rohn

Ya…I'm not a fan of bullies. Arrogant, unapproachable, interruptive, judgmental, narcissistic, short-tempered, unappreciative, and unforgiving personalities are found in every business, and *man, do they need Maintenance!*

Sometimes we can be intimidated by someone's education, financial and/or social status, physical appearance or their mere presence. However, we all have something to contribute to this life. We all need each other; especially women—to learn, uplift, and encourage each other. When we have an accomplishment, we get excited, when we have a loss of any kind, we feel pain and sadness. Every person has a story. We may never know all the joys and disappointments someone has been through. Retreats release the temptation to judge. Retreats bring stories together.

Debby Gibson (Colorado), Area Manager Park Lane Jewelry, Retreat Attendee

MOTIVATION

Goal: Build stronger relationships through team play.

Team play can be a specific sport or activity, either by working together or in separate groups. The idea is to have fun while taking them *slightly* out of their comfort zone where they can experience a little vulnerability. Pretenses fade, relationships are built, and friendships are created during this element. Motivation releases anxiety and opens the door to trust.

The Law of Influence
Your influence is determined by how abundantly you place other peoples' interest first.

The Go-Giver

Personal Reflection

IT'S TIME TO MAKE A MOVE!

I left the medical field when my fourth child was born. I was a stay-home mom for twelve years, and then rejoined the workforce in direct sales—something I knew nothing about! Nothing was familiar except the female to male ratio, much like my own nest of five girls to one boy. The company was young, filled with opportunities, and I was eager to begin a new and flexible career.

Every month, leaders were updated with their rank based on their team volume or production. I was stuck in the middle, 17 out of 35. For years, my team rank didn't budge. There was another leader, however, who was very familiar with the number one position. Once in a while she'd slip to number two, but when the annual conference came around, Margo still received the highest award.

The organization roared with applause when Margo walked onto the stage to accept her trophy. Team leaders crowded around and embraced her with congratulations. Every heart was sincere, but also determined to achieve the award the following year, myself included.

Soon after one particular conference, I took time to reassess my goals. If I wanted to be among the top echelon in the company, then I had to sharpen my skills. My mission was to absorb what I could from Margo and to observe her interactions. So, in the middle of a very cold winter, I packed up my car and drove across the country to attend her new product release event.

Margo was magnetic and powerful. Her smiles were spilling over everyone in her path. She went out of her way to make me feel comfortable, as if I were the most important person in the room.

I was taken aback. Margo was free to lead with her heart, something my manager warned me against. She carved out time for each team member and even made friends with strangers in the next room. Margo is a dynamic woman, and I left knowing just why her team was number one. She initiated a playful spirit, and her team joined in on the fun.

A company depends on productivity, but it swiftly became clear to me that leadership was more than a numbers game. A team is a hungry unit of real people, and people yearn to belong. They want someone to care about their success. Margo knew how to nurture her team and make them feel like family. Leaders require more knowledge than what's written in a procedure manual; their team desires, and needs, a genuine relationship, a connection to believe in something bigger than the product.

An immediate shift took place. I began to listen and lead with my heart, trusting that relationships within my team were naturally growing. I no longer fought my instincts. I was having fun; *we* were having fun. *Serving the needs of my team became one of my reasons to lead.* Within six months, we jumped from #17 to #5 in the company!

SECOND NOTE TO SELF: Listen to your gut. If your leadership style is not working, then find another mentor!

Motivation inspires.

HOW TO MOTIVATE:
How to Play!

The theme of one of my most powerful retreats came from the movie *Hook*, which is intertwined in the message throughout the rest of this book. We often forget who we are and where to find our joy. We grow up, get old, and take on more responsibilities than we should. We become depressed, wonder how we got to where we are with so little to show for all our hard work. Did we ever become who we wanted to be?

Leaders can lose their vision, especially when they take on more and more responsibilities. Retreats provide a creative group setting in which to retrieve and set new goals. They are a collective time to re-energize and re-focus as a company. When we change the perspective to think as a team, for the team, *for the better of the company,* we multiply blazing behaviors and everyone leaves a winner.

In 1991 Steven Spielberg directed a new twist of Peter Pan in the movie, Hook.

Peter Banning (the adult Peter Pan) and his family visit Granny Wendy in England. (Wendy, who is now a grandmother.) Captain Hook kidnaps Peter's children, holding them ransom until the battle resumes between Hook and Peter Pan. Peter must return to Neverland and rediscover his youthful spirit in order to fight Hook and save his children, but Peter forgot how to play.

If you can't imagine yourself being Peter Pan, you WON'T be Peter Pan! —Tink

What happens to our Pan? What happens to the child within us when responsibilities and economies start crumbling? What happens when we lose our jobs and can't pay our mortgage; when we lose our health or someone we love, and can't seem to smile again? We certainly don't want to play, and if anyone invited us to do so, we'd mumble, 'I'm just not in the mood.'

Motivation *is* play; it's the games that sustain momentum. Motivation is what moves a team onward and upward, but it isn't as effective if you don't do the Maintenance first. Before a team begins to move, it's vital to understand where you are going and why. Maintenance allows external layers to melt so that you can invite creativity and action with ease.

Great leadership begins with your own inspiration and how you personally connect with your team. The company you work for or represent does not stifle your inner leadership desire. They may govern the policies, but you control the passion in your heart. Upper management may instruct you to follow a manual, but they cannot stop you from gaining individual trust, smiling at an employee, or sending out a birthday card.

After Captain Hook abducts Peter's children, Granny Wendy tells him who he really is and of his need to return to Neverland. Tink (Tinker Bell) pays Peter a visit to encourage him to confront Hook. Unfortunately, Peter does not cooperate. He is in total disbelief and denial of the fact that he could ever have been Peter Pan.

Peter wrestles with Tink. He trips and falls unconscious, but Tink won't give up on the Pan she knows so well. She wraps him up in a blanket and with her mighty strength (for such a little bug), carries Peter out the open window toward the 'second star on the right, and on til' morning.'

Leaders are Tinks. We are the encouragers and our teams' greatest fan. Without cheering and building a community of support, we wouldn't be leaders. Without offering training and a means of communication, we wouldn't have a team. We would be isolated and probably drive ourselves bonkers from boredom. When we work and live alone, we're the only conversation that's happening.

Mind chatter is constantly running its mouth. What we think and say in our heads equals 550 words per minute. I didn't count, and I doubt Brian Tracy did either, but in his book *Unlimited Sales Success (2013)*, he did the research. We speak 480,000 words a day to ourselves. What are you talking yourself into? Never let the negativity of others become your reality. The most influential conversation you have every day is with yourself.

Both women and men enjoy comradery and can be encouraging friends to each other. Women make efforts to schedule free time for shopping, eating, catching a movie, or planning a weekend getaway with their BFF. Men typically enjoy their fishing and golf trips, pumping iron, and hanging with the guys for Monday Night Football. In his book *Love Does*, Bob Goff writes, "God doesn't always hand us audible answers to our prayers, but He does hand us each other."

Children know such a lot now. Soon they don't believe. And every time a child says, "I don't believe in fairies, there's a fairy someplace that falls down dead." —Tink

Tink falls as a result of Peter's boisterous claim that he doesn't believe in fairies. Tink tells Peter to keep clapping, louder and louder because it's the only thing that will save her.

Being an encourager is a natural attribute for humans, but even leaders can forget how to 'be a fan.' We love applause, but sometimes we, too, forget to clap.

During a professional sports game there are occasional lulls of silence in the stands. Players lift and wave their arms, spurring for more noise. What happens? An explosion of cheer rises from the crowd! Fans come alive, subsequently roaring the team to life!

Leaders are fans who believe in their team, and they can prove this through giving recognition, praise, and awards. Break the silence; instill a reward program in your department. If your company doesn't offer one, start one on your own.

That which is recognized is repeated. —Anonymous

Praise generates more praise. Allow your team to succeed. Don't let your team fall. You hold the power to lift, engage, and motivate them. You are their Tink. Sometimes you need to clap louder than other times, but always keep clapping. Sometimes, you need to wrap them up in a blanket and carry them away to a place where they can remember how to play.

During retreats, my team leaders play. I'm in tune to their giggles, and I watch them find their joy. Retreats provide a welcoming atmosphere filled with grace. Attendees become life-long friends and fiercely encourage each other, just like Tink.

National managers, regional directors, field managers, supervisors, leaders who support a down-line, department, or team; we all know it can be lonely at the top. Leadership is a service role for the prosperity of the team. When we come to believe in this, we understand that often we are our own cheerleader and need to provide our own 'pixie dust.'

Sprinkle away!

Have you ever thought of yourself as The Encourager for your team? If not, why?

_____

_____

_____

_____

If so, give some examples of how you boost team morale.

_____

_____

_____

_____

_____

_____

_____

_____

_____

Observe your team. The next time someone in your department or team achieves even the smallest task, joyfully encourage him/her by showing praise!

Make a list of rewards you will use to encourage your team: (cards, candy, or snacks make great little rewards!)

_____

_____

_____

_____

_____

_____

_____

_____

The element of Motivation was an outdoor activity and a bit outside of my comfort zone. As a team player though, I gave it my best until I fell. I got up, cleaned the dust off my knees, and planted a smile of confidence on my face. As I went to clean up, I had the most amazing revelation: Sometimes in our journey we fall, but when we get up, we have the opportunity to come back stronger than what we were before. When a team is there for support, we are lifted even higher. Retreats allow us to realize this and work harder together.

Francisca Kear (Colorado), Independent Marketing Director, Team National, Retreat Attendee

THE PLEASANT, BUT NOT PRESENT, LEADER

Corporations across the world are flooded with people holding a leadership title without any understanding or respect for the role. Graham Snowdon, from *The Guardian* (2012), wrote: "According to a report by the Resolution Foundation, the phenomenon of job title inflation has been growing in recent years, which is to say there is an increasing proportion of people who have senior-sounding job titles but who still earn middle-ranking wages." A leadership title can be a displacement or a process, an over-crowded level of management as individuals are waiting for *anything* to open. Some of these leaders are not equipped to take the risks and challenges their position necessitates. They are mere puppets to upper management and governed by their actions. Still, others are qualified, but uncomfortable in their position and rattled when it comes to actually serving a team. Either way, there are too many employees being given a leadership title. Sometimes this scenario gets in the way of engagement, and ultimately interferes with production.

Brenda is a Revenue and Receipts Coordinator for a major health care provider in the Midwest. Like all companies, production powers the business, and in Brenda's department, this couldn't be more reinforced. Like most businesses, the department head is solely focused on the outcome, and has nothing to do with the forty co-workers who provide the numbers.

The leader isn't a scrooge, in fact, employees believe she's pleasant. She sits behind her desk and sends an occasional smile through the office window, but she's not really present. There is no personal connection, no team interaction, and no attempt to build trust. Employees like Brenda spend eight hours every day in a cubicle, punching in numbers, wishing they were somewhere else. Does this sound familiar?

Brenda's job performance is measured by quotas (how much she produces). If daily numbers aren't met, a written warning gets tucked into her personal file. Sick days, arriving late to work, or leaving early (with a legitimate excuse or not) are also non wavering warnings that get added to her file. Six warnings within a year, and she would be handed the pink slip. There's nothing about her job that is engaging or appealing. Here's the part of our conversation that really caught my interest: Every year the HR (Human Resource) department is required to send out a morality survey to get feedback from the employees. *Talk about walking into the lion's den!* Any insight to what the results to this survey might be? You might be able to take an educated guess, but no one ever really knows. Year after year the polls continue, but nothing seems to get better. It's no wonder people loathe going to work. Does their voice really matter?

Years prior, Brenda was a supervisor in the accounting division for Sears. At that time, Personnel Departments (PD) were the liaison between employees and management. Once a week Brenda was required by the PD to call each employee into her office, spend five minutes building a rapport, going over their files and production numbers. This allotted time was a private, one on one discussion where both people could open up and talk about anything. Although most PD supervisors were intimidating to sit with, Brenda took a more personal approach, inquiring about personal goals and acknowledging achievements. Any thoughts as to what a return survey might look like if Brenda sent one out to her team?

Margaret Naughton, HR Administrator for a mining and construction company, explains how many HR departments have moved away from the old school idea of "rules police" and into the role of business partner. "HR departments now have the opportunity to encourage employee engagement by offering mentoring programs, teaching the art of coaching, and creating employee development plans, for instance. Providing tools and programs such as these to all employees creates a culture that allows leaders to lead and makes employee engagement an everyday occurrence. Everybody wins!"

Not everyone has access to great HR. Their role is a balancing act between being an advocate for the employee and an advocate as a business partner for the company. Often they're pleasant, but far from being present to satisfy employee conflicts. According to Ms. Naughton, there are HR departments who have leaders setting the tone to build better relationships with each person by offering individual development plans to enhance skills and job security. This new trend could help fill the leadership development void we have today.

In the meantime, developing future leaders is in the hands of today's current leaders in any department and at any level. However, some leaders and managers simply aren't qualified to be in their position. What if the leader is more comfortable as a follower, or what if he or she knows they won't be there long? In cases like these, it's easy to see why there's little attempt to help develop the team. Perhaps the position wasn't properly filled in the first place. Hiring someone who isn't trained, or who fearfully fumbles when motivating a team, is adding to the 78% of disengaged employees (Gallup Poll).

Jim Clifton, Gallup Chairman and CEO, states,

> *"Leaders, here's something they'll probably never teach you in business school: The single biggest decision you make in your job—bigger than all of the rest—is who you name manager. When you name the wrong person manager, nothing fixes that bad decision. Not compensation, not benefits—nothing."*

Leaders, would you want to work for another leader, supervisor, or manager who was inept—never present or indifferent to your existence? What if you *did* have a leader who engaged in a daily conversation or provided a small token of appreciation, like Brenda? Wouldn't it bring a sense of synergy to the workplace? I bet you would feel a little more like a valued human than a droid living in a cubicle.

Dustin Thomas works in IT as a field service representative. He says there's a difference between managers and bosses. "These titles are as different as 'job' and 'career.' I was having my annual review with my manager and he said something very interesting that his manager told him years ago. 'I'm not your boss. A boss tells you what to do at your job and you do it. I'm your manager. I'll help guide you and manage your career.' That's how I lead in my position today. Not everyone wants to be told what to do; people want to understand why they do it—they want to visualize the difference it will make in the end."

You can be the leader or manager who mentors others. When you start building trusting relationships and start utilizing individual strengths, you will see a natural progression of production. This approach empowers the individual, transforms the team, and the entire organization. Leadership can begin with you!

As a leader, you have incredible influence over your team. You might be pleasant, but unless you're approachable and willing to engage, no one will follow. Start something great. Open your office door; start a conversation. Be present.

What personal virtues do you hold in the highest regard?
What is it about yourself that you won't compromise as a
person and as a leader?

_____

_____

_____

_____

_____

What happens when those virtues are compromised or
threatened? How do you feel and how do you react?

_____

_____

_____

_____

_____

_____

_____

What are some of the virtues individuals in your department or team value?
Are they the same as yours?

_____

_____

_____

_____

_____

_____

_____

_____

_____

Make an effort to leave your desk to start a conversation with someone in your department or team. Every day, reach out to someone new. Ask questions and listen. Then ask more questions…and listen.

Success is helping someone find joy, laughter and purpose in their journey

in order to reach their goals.

Colette French (Oregon), Network Development Representative,
Retreat Attendee

GROWING INTO A NEW ATTITUDE

Growing up is such a barbarous business, full of inconvenience and pimples.
—Hook

Peter Banning was required to think of his happy thought in order to fly and rescue his children. Unfortunately, he no longer believed in having fun or displaying a playful heart. He had no patience for the whimsical nature of youth. He was an adult now and to frolic in the past in order to think of his happy thought was pure folly.

What's a happy thought? I'm glad you asked.

Everyone has a happy thought. It's the drive deep inside your heart that makes you, *you*. It's your personal imprint and legacy which makes you special, unique, and good. It's the reason behind what you do. It's not a job description; it's a passion description.

A little attitude adjustment could change Peter's stubborn outlook, but how far will he risk what's at stake? Unless he takes the time to know his happy thought, he will lose his children to Hook. His ability to recall his happy thought is now the test of his life.

In order for Peter to collide with Pan, a personal retreat was necessary.

Peter's behavior is not uncommon in our culture. Times are tough. Economy remains sluggish, and the media constantly reminds us to live in fear. We're frail, and we break, and it takes hard work to heal. Do you know what the saddest part is? We don't want to play anymore.

The attitudes we choose drive our behavior and sometimes can drive the ones we love most right out of the picture, just like Peter Banning. When we feel lost, low, and at our whit's end, we must remember there are options. We can either change the physical situation or change our mindset to adapt to new circumstances. It's our responsibility to choose, but too often we're stuck thinking about it and too afraid to move one way or the other.

Taking forward steps is the ultimate goal, but leaving our comfort zone can be scary stuff. Sure it can be an exciting adventure, but getting there requires work. First, to reference Hook, it's inconvenient. Who has time to engage in a change? Sometimes, we'd rather settle and live in misery. Second, we like routine. We're comfortable in knowing outcomes. We don't like the unknown, or to enter into a clouded territory we can't see or control. We'd rather throw in the towel than do the dirty work that will get us through to the clearer side.

Leaders can step up to the plate and provide basic training for change. We have the ability to guide our team and reconnect to personal values and passion. We have the power to pull back and rejuvenate individual strength and team spirit in a safe environment.

"How do we hold tight to our beliefs and make choices from value rather than fear?" This question is hanging in my office. When fear becomes our stronghold, isn't it time to re-claim our virtues? Is it really convenient to extend our stay in camp misery?

Even when fear isn't practical, it uses logic to excuse itself.

There really are situations when fear is highly practical.

For instance, if you hear someone screaming, "Tamilyn, look out for that bear!" it's perfectly appropriate for your heart to beat a little faster. After all, you might need that adrenaline to run for your life.

If you're in the woods, that is.

But more often than not (for most of us) running for your life is more like running for your comfort zone.

And that, believe it or don't, isn't practical. —*Dixie Gillaspie,* Just Blow It Up: Firepower for Living an Unlimited Life

When life turns upside down (and it will), where are we supposed to find our joy? Falling down hurts and it's easier to run for cover. Life gets complicated and we lose sight of our passion. Sometimes, we even forget we had one.

What's your happy thought?

Change your attitude. Play. Come on...go for a little adventure!

What is your conscience telling you to do? Is it nudging you away from familiar territory? What does the outside of your comfort zone look like?

_____

_____

_____

_____

_____

_____

What is your happy thought?

_____

_____

_____

_____

_____

Your life is your journey and only you stop yourself from prevailing and moving forward to reach your goal. No matter what you're passionate about or what your goal is, don't let fear or self-doubt get in the way. Believe in yourself; sometimes you don't realize how much of an inspiration you are to others. You might change someone's life just by following through with your own journey!

Jules Abbott (Florida), Sales/Merchandising Supervisor Manager, Ralph Lauren, Retreat Attendee

PURPOSE

Goal: Discover a deeper, more confident self.

We are equipped to live a magnificent life, but sometimes we lose our direction. Leadership flows out of who we are, but anxiety can freeze our inhibitions to reach higher aspirations. Breaking through barriers can happen with a little help from thought activities.

The Law of Authenticity
The most valuable gift you have to offer is yourself.

The Go-Giver

Personal Reflection

PURPOSE: Google It!

There seems to be a winter-weather pattern associated with when I take my best moves forward. It was the morning of New Year's Eve and snow was piled high out the window. I hunkered down into a cozy chair with my laptop battery keeping me warm, reading about leadership seminars.

Like many of us, I was searching for deeper purpose, only I didn't know where to look. So I did what I tell all my children to do when seeking for an answer: "Google it!" As I was researching, my inbox was lit with an email from Bob Burg. The message was an e-blast to thousands of followers letting us know about his upcoming leadership seminar. At that time, I only knew Mr. Burg as the co-author of *The Go-Giver*, the powerful book I gift to my team leaders. I never could have imagined the ground-breaking experience that was coming up before me.

His conference was one of a kind, truly enlightening. I got to meet Bob and fell smitten with his candor. His guest speakers were top notch, intoxicating the room with wisdom. All I had to do was to reach out and grab some; any of it would get me started on a more meaningful path. So I did. I reached out and met Dixie Gillaspie, a mentor, coach, and now, sweet friend.

According to the many books I've read, the most successful leaders live an authentic life, both in business and in their personal endeavors. Balance comes from finding peace within both work and life. I wasn't feeling a sense of peace, but I wasn't looking to find any, either. I wanted to take off and find purpose and success. After all, I'm a doer. Just to feel as though I was moving was better than standing still. Yet, that's exactly why I couldn't move forward; I needed to grow *in* before I could grow *out*.

"Thoughts are born in the mind, feelings are born in the heart, knowing is born in the soul." —Dixie Gillaspie

Discovering the power of our soul drives us to our purpose. We want to believe our life has meaning and that we are born to make a positive change in the world. As leaders, we want to believe we are that impact. When we don't see results, our hearts become discouraged. We start to beat ourselves up, believing we're not good enough to lead.

Yuk.

I was searching for a long time for to find the ultimate success. To be a leader is awesome, but was I really making a difference or was I simply trying to feed my own ego? Was my heart hungry to serve others, or was my head just missing accolades?

Ouch.

Are you leading because it makes you feel powerful and in charge, or are you leading because you are empowering and serving others to reach a united goal? One moves the world forward and the other one, well, doesn't. I often wonder if we've been asking the wrong question to our children; instead of 'What do you want to do -or who do you want to be when you grow up?' we should be encouraging, 'Who—and how—do you want to serve others when you grow up?' Serving satisfies the soul. Maybe they would embrace more fulfillment at a younger age if we took this approach.

Over the years, many authors and internet searches have sent me on quests and journeys into the heart with hopes of defining my strength, but I was never satisfied with the results these resources offered. The truth is, I wanted to move the world and serve others, but I didn't know how. After Mr. Burg's event, I forced myself to slow down for self-reflection.

After re-reading some of my old pathway-to-purpose books, I finally decided to craft an exercise of my own that would help me define my value, my vision, and my contribution to others. I designed on paper what I really wanted to accomplish, and when I defined and read the true intention of my heart it was the ultimate 'aha' moment.

Since I believe revelations are for sharing, I turned these notes into a book, my first published work titled, *Authentic Purpose*. I wrote it for myself—and I wrote it for you, too. You see, I'm not so different than you. Maybe by the reflection in the mirror I am, but there are times each of us craves for a deeper meaning in life; we wonder why life has to be so hard, and we often struggle with which path to take. Well, there's no better feeling than to follow the one with your name written on the signpost!

The concept of Authentic Purpose is about serving God and each other while we're here. Like the wind, however, our direction in life changes. Acknowledging our purpose allows us to pursue our passion with a fervent plan, but we can't always follow the same road for an entire lifetime. There are many different chapters and challenges filled with experiences—early childhood, education, career, raising a family—that require specific devotions. Our strengths often change, and our desires do, too, physically and mentally.

We need to invite opportunities for new growth and new direction until God decides to take us home. Therefore, it is wise to take personal time-outs to 'grow in;' to balance purpose, feed passion, and renew direction.

THIRD NOTE TO SELF: God was right, I do have a purpose.

Purpose clarifies.

My first and only experience with a leadership retreat was wonderful. I had a chance to interact with other leaders, and we all shared a lot of valuable information on how to succeed. The training we had helped me to keep focused on my goals, and to overcome some challenges in my business. Most importantly, our training was very interactive and fun, and helped me to understand better what I should do as a leader to create a strong team. This leadership retreat definitely gave me more motivation to keep going, have a purpose, and plan my success. I really had a great time, and I'm looking forward to the next one!

Dr. Jamaria Martins (Wisconsin), Research Scientist, Retreat Attendee

TAMILYN BANNO

IDENTITY CRISIS

Peter, don't you know who you are? —Granny Wendy

How often do you question your purpose? How many times do you question your current business path or leadership skills? These are very popular questions; just cruise through the self-help section in any book store and gaze through the many shelves filled with endless titles. We all wonder. We wonder so much, it hurts.

Our purpose is guided by our inner spiritual strength. When we don't pay attention to it, we feel lost and feel a lack of fulfillment. Eventually, we can slip into a field of self-doubt that can spiral us into a maze of fear. When this happens, recapturing our purpose can take time and can involve *feelings*. Many people would rather not venture into the realm of deep seeded emotions.

Valuing ourselves is necessary to move forward, but in order to do so, we have to do the work. There's a beacon of love inside us; it just depends how much we want it lit. Many of us say we wish we had a more meaningful life, but do we really work at having a better life? All too often we stop the effort. As we get older, too much time has passed and we've learned to accept the regret of not fulfilling our dreams. We lose faith in a better life; we lose strength to keep up the fight; and we lose the passion we had when we once really cared.

In the movie, Hook, *Peter turned to the police upon learning his children were kidnapped. Granny Wendy, however, turned to the book on her nightstand titled* Peter Pan. *She opened the cover and showed a picture to Peter. Annoyed and confused at the timing of her intent, Peter stretched his patience to give her attention. Granny glared into his eyes and said, "Peter, don't you know who you are?"*

Where does the heart of childhood go? What happens to the giggles and uncontrollable belly laughs? When does the sense of adventure leave our souls? What about all the questions we asked as annoying toddlers? When did we lose our inquisitive minds? We must have plenty of wonder left in us, so why do we feel so disengaged?

Childlike attitudes used to absorb our perceptions and imaginations. A dishtowel around our shoulders transformed us into Superman. Crayon drawings of lions jumped from the page with ear-piercing ROARS. Our two-bedroom homes were mansions in disguise with secret doors leading to secret gardens and hiding places (like mom could never see us scrambling under the open legs of a kitchen chair during hide and seek). Dads were friendly giants, way bigger than *anything* in the world, and everyone had a scary relative that provided plenty of nightmares (wait…that one still might be true).

When did a dish towel become a *dish towel*? What happened to the secret doors that lead us into spectacular gardens? When did we turn out to be the same, having the same struggles of being over-worked and overwhelmed? When did life get so busy and so stressful, depriving us of adventure? I wonder at what age I was considered a grownup and banned from Neverland. Was it an age or an attitude?

"There are different kinds of bravery and Mr. Darling put away many dreams." Michael asked, "Where does he put them?" Mrs. Darling replied, "In a drawer. Sometimes we take them out at

night, but it gets harder to close the drawer; that's bravery." —
Peter Pan

In my opinion, that's sad.

I don't know where you are in your life, but I can bet you have a drawer full of dreams. When was the last time you opened it to let one fly out? There's no better time to breathe life into a dream than the present.

When there's a smile in your heart, there's no better time to start. —Tink

We are all Lost Boys, orphans in the wild terrains of life. When we live outside of our joy for any length of time, we wander and sometimes we can't find our way home. Retreats provide the atmosphere to reclaim our identity. They are opportunities for inner perspective, adventure, and growth. What defines us is strengthened by the love buried in our hearts. Retreats reveal our buried treasure.

Great leaders are in tune with the growth and changing aspirations of their team. Retreats provide the opportunity to adjust the flight plan accordingly. Peter lost his joy and didn't have a clue how to get it back, but Tink, the encourager, did. She took him on a retreat.

Fairies are so cool!

So are team leaders.

Peter's true values became clear again when he took the time to see them. Allow your team to see theirs, too. Retreats are gifts that stir the soul.

What's one of your dreams? What's another one? (Both personal and business)

Personal

_____

_____

_____

_____

_____

Business

_____

_____

_____

_____

_____

What small step could you take today toward one of your dreams?

Personal

_____

_____

_____

_____

_____

_____

_____

Business

_____

_____

_____

_____

_____

_____

Who encourages you, and how?

_____

_____

_____

_____

_____

_____

_____

What qualities do you think your team sees in you that allows

them to believe in your purpose and passion?

_____

_____

_____

_____

_____

_____

_____

_____

Reading and taking the Authentic Purpose exercise helped me redefine and refocus my passion. Deep down, I knew what my passion was, but I didn't take the time to identify it. I needed to, but I didn't know I needed to. I believe I'm a much better teacher and leader since I was able to identify and focus that passion.

Michelle Mayer (Illinois), BAE/BOMA

LOST AND FOUND

Oh, THERE you are, Peter! —Lost Boy

It's fun to reminisce and recall how much we played as children. As I recall, we slipped in attending school *around* our neighborhood escapades; swinging at the corner park, conjuring up a game of street ball, and belting out an occasional song by Peter, Paul, and Mary. Good memories warm the heart. Life in general, however, seems to weather our bones—and weather our souls, too.

In the movie Hook, *Tink brought Peter to the Lost Boys for help. He needed to find his 'happy thought' in order to reveal his purpose. Tink knew the boys could help stir his soul. Unfortunately, they didn't believe he could possibly be Peter Pan. First of all, he was a grown-up, and Peter promised never to grow up. Second of all, he was too fat to be the Pan. One of the littlest Lost Boys, however, kept his wonder. He tugged and tugged at Peter's shirt until Peter finally looked down and knelt beside him.*

The boy took off Peter's glasses and studied his face. He pulled back Peter's aging skin, playing with it like Play Dough, trying to expose any characteristics of the Pan. A few moments later the boy's face lit up, "Oh, there you are, Peter!" he exclaimed.

I'm not sure what you do in the morning while getting ready for the day. Like the little Lost Boy, I often look in mirror, pull back my skin and finally discover, 'Oh, hey, there you are!' Then I release my grip and convince myself (at least for the moment) that I earned every wrinkle and I'm proud to wear each one. Then, I hunt for the anti-aging cream and ultimate wrinkle cover base in my makeup bag.

Regardless of our age, we need to play, on purpose. Our spirits are ageless, but we often forget how to release that energy. We have every excuse not to engage; "There's too much to do!" "I'm too old", or "I'm too depressed", but there's a life inside of us jumping for joy. We owe it to ourselves to encourage a playful spirit and live with more adventure before our adventure ends.

What were your favorite games to play as a child?

_____

_____

_____

_____

_____

What things made you laugh out loud?

_____

_____

_____

_____

_____

Allow yourself to play today.
Oh, and throw in a good belly laugh!

TAMILYN BANNO

YOUR VOICE MATTERS

Every individual brings his or her own experience to the team. Behind the experience lays a human heart and each one has a story of brokenness. Through retreats, broken pieces come together. As leaders, we get to help; we get to listen, learn, and shape others by our words of encouragement. Retreats give us that place of opportunity.

In any organization there's a breeding ground of people not feeling appreciated. No matter how hard a leader tries, not every moment is golden and not every person will be a team player. Everyone, however, deserves compliments and when the compliments are genuine, trust will inch into the relationship.

Some leaders don't grasp the importance of listening. Some get caught up in a handful of tasks and assume their unspoken words are understood. Words change us; they can build us up or tear us down. The scary part is, we are all responsible for what we say and how our words affect people.

We live in a beauty obsessed culture where self-loathing and bullying fill the school halls and internet. Many children suffer in silence, and a few end up taking their own lives. The power of words can inspire or devastate a soul.

What words are you saying to your team? The old "sticks and stones may break my bones, but names will never hurt me" cliché is just not true. Names hurt, and unspoken words can hurt even more.

Kathy has been working in advertising for over 30 years. As you can imagine, her experience and integrity are superior to most others in her department. She is held in high regard by her peers and company officers. Upper management tends to leave her alone when it comes to daily projects. In fact, they don't say much at all; four words over the last two years have been spoken in Kathy's direction. No engaging conversations, just a random 'Hey, how ya' doin' kind of thing.

Contrary to what people may believe, even senior leaders, department heads, and Vice President's require acknowledgment. Hearing nothing only increases our mind chatter, and you know where that can lead.

Jill Geisler, in a 2012 article in *Poynter.org*, recalls the answer managers give when asked the secret to success:

> *"'Hire good people and get out of their way.' That phrase, and variations on it, fly in the face of truly good management. I know some bosses use it in a self-effacing way, suggesting their people are so talented they barely need a boss, or as an earnest rejection of micromanagement."*

From the boss' perspective, Kathy's reputation preceded her, so her superior's attention is focused elsewhere. Regardless, it's misleading. We all want to know and to be reminded we're doing a good job. Everyone wants to be commended and proudly recognized for their accomplishments. Jill continues, "They don't want to be left alone to figure out how they matter to the organization, what they're doing well, or what they could do to get even better."

My oldest daughter is pursuing her doctorate in clinical psychology. In her first year she began to write her thesis; I thought she was going to pull her hair out in frustration. Weeks of editing turned into long drawn-out months of writing and re-writing per the endless red ink that blotted her work. It took a solid year of stress and self-doubt before her mentor gave an encouraging word. When he did, her whole perspective changed; her determination was renewed and, shortly after, her thesis was successfully defended.

Listening strengthens relationships, as do the words we choose. In your next conversation with a team member, listen intently. Take time to make it all about the person speaking. Listen as if you're hearing for the first time. Knowing where the other person is coming from is powerful knowledge and a sign of a stellar leader.

Listen to everyone you meet today. Listen with your eyes and your heart, as well as your ears.

Journal what you heard.

BEING THERE

When people want your attention, they need both ears and the space in between. Sometimes they just want to let their voice be heard, get emotions out, and to solve their own problems. Years back I remember one of my daughters ranting and raving over a conflict at school. I tried every which way to offer a solution when suddenly she shut me up and wailed, "Mom, stop! Let me vent!" That's when I realized that sometimes people just want to be heard. They don't necessarily want a solution; they want to circumvent their emotions and have them validated. My role was to just listen.

Different levels of listening range from ignoring the person who is speaking to empathetically paying attention. Several charts and graphs have been authored by respected psychologists over the years. The steps I follow actually come from the four levels of Jewish interpretation of scriptures; Pardes.

The rules of Pardes interpretation is known by its acronyms, PRDS. When translated from Hebrew to English, they become SHSH. Each layer goes deeper into the meaning of the context. When I apply the process to listening and understanding, I focus immediately by just saying, "Shhh Shhh" in my mind. This keeps me from interrupting and triggers me to re-gain eye *and ear* contact.

Pashat…in Hebrew means SIMPLE
Remez…in Hebrew means HINT
Drash…in Hebrew means SEARCH
Sod…in Hebrew means HIDDEN

Pashat is the simple meaning of the text; it's the process of hearing that someone needs my attention. When a serious conversation begins, my eyes focus on the subject. *Remez* reveals a deeper meaning of the text. This is when I really start to pay attention to the mood behind the words. *Drash* begins to put verses together. This is where empathy genuinely kicks in, and I try with all my might to feel and understand the same emotions as the one who is speaking. *Sod* is the hidden secret of the text. It's when I study the emotions, especially anger, bitterness, and envy. Sink into the conversation; tune in to what's really being said.

There are many people who are impatient listeners. I've often heard, 'If the person can't tell me what they really mean, it's their loss, not mine.' I believe it takes skill to be articulate, and that this is something many of us are never able to fully master.

Often, there is a bigger story behind what's being said; just knowing that much helps me to be a more compassionate listener. Perhaps because I'm one of those who can't always articulate my thoughts clearly, I tend to listen more intently. I don't have to agree with the person, but I do have to get into their heads to understand their point of view. Great leaders are patient in understanding, even if they don't agree.

As a leader, communication begins with YOU. Listen, really, really listen, and sink your feet into their shoes. Try to understand the unspoken words and emotions that aren't coming through. When you are not present or become unavailable, they'll find someone else (even another leader) to hear them, or they might lose interest in the business altogether.

Heated conversations are inevitable. Every day at work and at home, we're bound to witness, or to be involved in, a quarrel. The one who continually interrupts has the least control over the conversation, the one who lets go of the stronghold point of view has the most control of the conversation, and the person who listens with an empathetic heart owns the conversation.

Which listener are you? Do you often interrupt? (Do you realize you interrupt?)
Is your opinion more important than theirs? Explain.

During your next conversation, concentrate on the person and the emotion behind the story. What's REALLY being said?

FULFILLMENT

Peter, you are missing IT! —Moira

Peter's wife, Moira, is frustrated with Peter's work schedule and lack of family commitment. He is missing the gift of fatherhood and Moira keeps warning him over and over again, "Peter, you are missing IT!"

We miss IT. Every day of every week throughout our lives we miss something and disappoint ourselves or someone we love. Overtime at work causes us to miss dinner. Rush hour traffic keeps us from our children's dance recital. Missing the due dates on the bills increases our debt. Through all our efforts, we never quite fill the need required by our family, friends, and co-workers and unfortunately, never quite quench our own desires. We think we know what we want and when we get it, we end up wanting something different, or even wanting more.

Kenneth Behring is a successful entrepreneur, but he wasn't born with a silver spoon in his mouth. In fact, it was quite the contrary. His life is a true rags to riches story. Ken grew up during the Great Depression, but through his determination and tenacity he rose above poverty and worked hard from one fruitful adventure to another. When he made it big owning several car dealerships, he ventured into real-estate.

After that turned golden, he bought a professional football team. However, Ken never felt fulfilled; his thirst for more was addicting. At least it was until he found purpose in life.

In his book *Road to Purpose*, Ken states,

"I deeply regret wasting so many years before finding purpose—not because I lacked the desire to find what I was looking for, but because I started out thinking it would come through financial achievement."

Ken finally found purpose when he touched the life of another person. In 1999, he flew in his private jet overseas to deliver medical supplies. As a favor for another medical mission, he dropped off a few wheelchairs to a Romanian hospital on his way back to the states. This special delivery changed the course of Ken's life.

As mobile as Ken's life was, he never appreciated the gift of mobility until he met an elderly man who had suffered a stroke and couldn't walk anymore. After witnessing the man's tears of gratitude for the wheelchair, Ken was struck with humility and compassion.

"People in poor and developing countries with physical disabilities are discarded. They often aren't treated as human beings. As a result of their illnesses or inability to move, they and their families are stigmatized...In many parts of the world, the disabled are treated as if they are cursed or possessed by evil spirits...They are hidden away in the back of a hut and given a single daily meal. Sometimes their families are ashamed to see them crawl or be carried, so they lock them away. I have seen people in boxes in back rooms."

The gift of wheelchairs penetrated the heart of Ken more than any other act of kindness or business success he experienced. Ken immediately started the Wheelchair Foundation, which continues today, donating chairs to the underprivileged around the world.

Ken had known something important was missing from his life, but it wasn't until he received joy from the tangible gift of giving, and giving to the most forgotten people on earth, that he found the fulfillment that made his life complete.

"You don't have to be rich, own big houses or planes, travel, or know famous people to do something good for someone else. You can start out small, like I did—one wheelchair for one person, one act of kindness for one person, one smile for one person, maybe just once a month, or with just one percent of your time. With purpose, we can change the world."

No matter how much we have, our hearts are empty until we experience fulfillment and realize our purpose. How will you know? Trust me, *you'll know*.

It is extremely important to understand why one exists, as it brings a sense of fulfillment. The greatest task for any person is to find meaning in his or her life. One knows if he or she is living life on purpose when there's passion.

We are more than our careers, more than a title or more than what others may say that we are. Purpose is the fuel that ignites the fire within us. It's what gives us the sense of direction and our reason for living.

Carolyn G. Anderson (Wisconsin), Executive Coach, Retreat Attendee

Discover your purpose by participating in the Authentic Purpose exercise in the workbook available on my website (TamilynBanno.com). When your statement is complete, write it below.

_____

_____

_____

_____

_____

_____

Write the vision statement of the company where you work.

(If you don't know what it is, ask!)

_____

_____

_____

_____

_____

How are the two statements alike?

_____

_____

_____

_____

_____

_____

_____

_____

_____

_____

_____

_____

_____

_____

_____

_____

PLAN

Goal: Design your tomorrow.

Map out a path toward the bigger goal together with your team. When everyone sees the visualization of the target and has a say in how to get there, teamwork is at its best. A great way to keep a plan on track is through comradery and communication.

The Law of Compensation
Your income is determined by how many people you serve and how well you serve them.

The Go-Giver

TAMILYN BANNO

Personal Reflection

TURN UP THE HEAT!

As I write this, would you believe it's not only winter again, but the coldest day recorded in 20 years? No road trips planned; my car is frozen.

In the dead of winter my sales team seems to slow down a few notches. After the holiday rush many of the top leader's crash, myself included. In fact, I close the door to my home office for a few days, but not much longer than that; I don't want my team to lose motivation.

Despite the weather, when the temperature of a team drops, the leader needs to turn up the heat. Leaders have the ability to improve business performance by encouraging creativity and communication. If a team is fortunate, they have a leader who's a caring mentor and will keep them motivated, nurture their strengths, and acknowledge their achievements, especially when they need a little fire lit under their feet.

My love and respect grew as my team developed. For nearly three years, I held the number three position in the company. I was still keen on achieving number one, but my approach concentrated on their needs and promotions. Their success meant as much to me as my own and, at times, more.

The plan for my first retreat was reserved for the top seven team leaders. The goal was to develop a stronger bond through the four elements of Maintenance, Motivation, Purpose, and Plan. The experience ended up changing the dynamics and position of the team. Spirits were motivated, and momentum took off!

Near the end of the retreat, I declared my vision for the team. Together, we would achieve the next level of directorship within 90 days. This would definitely be a challenge. I knew the numbers, and if you're in sales, you know the game; goals take time, and this one wasn't feasible any earlier. At least, that's what I thought.

Within 30 days following the retreat, my leaders flowed into their new positions. This was an amazing feat since it required members of their own team to achieve higher rank, as well. This incredible shift promoted several leaders and enabled me to reach the first paid Regional Director in the company. Everyone who attended the retreat, including our National Sales Manager and Founder of the company, can attest to the fact that the retreat was *the* key factor in the promotions. The following year my team leaders doubled in size, and so did the attendance of the following retreats.

FOURTH AND FINAL NOTE TO SELF: Every year host an MMPP leadership retreat!

Plans execute.

A retreat is a great teaching tool. It teaches the importance of personal maintenance in order to relax and recharge our minds so we are on our game for faith, family, work, and friends. The element of motivation is fun. We realize our peers are walking with us on this journey and are there for support, wisdom, and encouragement. Purpose lets our creative hearts shine and points us in the right direction. Plan teaches us a format to build from and keeps us on task. Without a plan there is no further growth.

Cheryl Bjerke (Colorado), Fashion Stylist and Direct Sales Industry, Retreat Attendee

Plan your retreat by using the guidelines of Maintenance, Motivation, Purpose, and Plan.

What do you want to celebrate with your team?

_____

What training do you want to focus on during the retreat?

_____

_____

_____

_____

Begin with Maintenance; List ideas for personal reflection

and/or care.

_____

_____

_____

_____

Motivation; List ideas for a little outdoor exercise or excursion, keeping your theme, celebration, and training topics in mind.

_____

_____

_____

_____

_____

_____

Purpose; Take time for the Authentic Purpose exercise. This valuable tool brings passion to life by offering better clarity and direction.

Merge personal purpose with the company's vision to create a team vision. Do this as a group exercise using a flip chart for ideas. Watch as the leaders brainstorm their ideas and take ownership in the goal.

Plan; Time is difficult to manage. It affects everyone and leads to stress and burn-out. There just aren't enough hours in a day. Take the opportunity to research the best program for your team, and train on time management during this session. Discuss the challenges and commitments for the techniques suggested. Have accountability partners to see goals to fruition.

TAMILYN BANNO

YOUR TEAM IS ALIVE!

To *live* would be an awfully big adventure! —Peter Pan

Many times we lose our way. We have fallen so hard that we believe God can't even save us, but we know He can and does. He breathed life into us and until He's ready to take it away, we must keep moving.

As a leader in your company, you are ridiculously in charge! According to Dr. Henry Cloud, in his book *Boundaries for Leaders*, you're not only in charge, you set the rules. You set the examples for team meetings, trainings, and recognitions, as well as boundaries on negativity. A great leader will ask the penetrating questions of what your team can and cannot control in order to break down the barriers that keep you from the flow of momentum. By your lead, your team recognizes its strengths and weaknesses while building and creating a path with direction and purpose.

Before a retreat, take the initiative to assess your team; are your team members engaged in the company? Have you taken the time to know both their personal and business goals? What anxieties and concerns get in the way of their production? What is keeping them from the risk of adventure to perform at a higher level? Leaders are able to sift through discouraging words and evaluate true capabilities. Making an impact with the *Purpose* element requires you to understand where your individual team leaders need the most help.

Years ago, Marianne Friedlund, the National Sales Manager of the organization I represented, relentlessly trained leaders to break through some pretty thick habits and attitudes in order to move us to the next level. It was a lot of work and even uncomfortable at times, but I came to realize she never believed we *couldn't* blast through; it was all about *when* we would blast through.

In the original movie, *Peter Pan*, Peter lives life on the edge, risking his life for the sole thrill of adventure. In our personal-life movies, we protect our adventures. If they require the element of risk, pretty likely, we'll skip the trip.

In the movie *Hook*, Peter Banning lost his sense of adventure; he was impatient, irritable, and even callous toward people. Once he returned to Neverland, Tink and the Lost Boys were able to guide him back to his center. Only then could he live life on the edge, risking adventures for the sole thrill of living! When Peter took the time to *be still*, he was able to pull energy from the inside to find his happy thought. It wasn't about *if* he could fly, it was all about *when*.

Your team is alive! They have vibrant personalities and vivid dreams, but some are hiding in dressers. Leaders can open up the drawers. What are the strengths each of your members bring to the team? Do you delegate and use their proficiencies to help with projects or train other members? Training upcoming leaders includes giving them the opportunity to take the reins. Supervise as they prepare and lead team meetings, let their leadership skills develop by allowing them to organize department newsletters, and letting them mentor new recruits or employees. Taking the fear out of a performance only comes with practice. You are in charge, and have a responsibility to guide them. Allow mistakes so that when the time comes, they can experience the thrill of a successful flight.

"A leader is one who knows the way, goes the way, and shows the way." —John Maxwell

In the beginning of the first retreat I held, leaders arrived as individuals, each flying a respected path. It was only after everyone left that we recognized we were on a new flight plan together, a flock, aligned and focused. No one recognized we were working on becoming a unit of strength; the elements of the retreat molded us into one and the experience wasn't anything less than Divine.

Retreats are for leaders and team members. They allow you to come together physically, emotionally, and spiritually. You come to find out that individual goals vary, but business challenges and goals tend to be related. Realizing this piece pulled us even closer. We were more alike than not.

Senior leaders have the opportunity to gather department leaders, break down the challenges, and build on the possible—not the impossible—solutions in order to achieve the ultimate vision.

Reignite the fire in your team and like magic, the difficult chunks will become bite size. There is an electric charge that generates from renewing the goals and the vision of an organization. Members feel empowered, and in a group setting walls begin to crumble, concrete starts to fly, and so do promotions. Retreats solidify purpose, direction, and trust, which lock in momentum. Then, when the leader engages in motivational plays, there's powerful movement—an effortless flow of energy toward the ultimate goal.

In the movie *Hook*, Peter couldn't fly until he discovered his happy thought. *More than anything in the world, Peter wanted to be a father.* Good thing he had Tink to bring him on a retreat and remind him of his passion!

Make use of the strengths within your team. Be present and faithful with rewards. Together you will arrive at the top and, as their leader, you wouldn't want it any other way.

"God put a million, million doors in the world for His love to walk through. One of those doors is you." —Jason Gray

What business goals do you want to achieve?

_____

_____

_____

_____

_____

_____

What are the goals of your team leaders? List what road
blocks hinder their achievement of these goals.

_____

_____

_____

_____

_____

_____

_____

What worries you most about achieving your goals?

How do (will) you encourage their leadership skills? (Lead team meetings, write newsletters, create a team-wide incentive, etc.)

A SURGE OF SUCCESS

Considerable research has shown that when individuals have a say in a company's value statement, they take ownership and responsibility to see it through. Nicole Alvino discusses employee commitment in the Forbes September 2014 article *Engage Your Employees or Lose Billions*. "What makes engaged employees different is that they are knowledgeable about their company's mission, and they tell the world what they and the company are up to." When a CEO or owner of an organization values the teams input, higher aspirations are often achieved. When a team pursues a statement that they had a hand in creating, they take ownership in the success of the company.

As an exercise during a retreat, hand out a blank card to each member. On one side, ask him or her to answer, "What is the company's vision?" On the other side have each one answer, "What is the goal of our team"? This little survey gives great insight into the knowledge of your department. If a person doesn't know where he is going, how can he know when he gets there?

Another great resource during this element is to address time management. We all struggle with appropriating time, and training materials are plentiful on this subject. My all-time favorite training is from Brian Tracy's book, *Eat That Frog!: 21 Great Ways to Stop Procrastinating and Get More Done in Less Time.* He says, "Mark Twain once said that if the first thing you do each morning is to eat a live frog, you can go through the day with the satisfaction of knowing that that is probably the worst thing that is going to happen to you all day long. Your "frog" is your biggest, most important task, the one you are most likely to procrastinate on if you don't do something about it. It is also the one task that can have the greatest positive impact on your life and results at the moment."

Everyone I know puts off that one phone call, that one conversation, that one closet to be cleaned, so I share this particular training every chance I get. Mapping out a daily routine is a helpful tool in starting your new tomorrow.

When we begin to take responsibility for our circumstances, success starts to roll. It's amazing how easy our walk becomes when we start a new goal without the default of blame on someone or something. There will always be road blocks and obstacles. Fear freezes our forward motion, but God never intended us to sit in one place. His purpose is to keep us moving; that's where success lives.

PLAN

Prepare your destination. With a company value statement in hand, work your way down to the team goal. Be sure all your leaders are on board with the plan. If your company does not have a value or vision statement, encourage them to design one. In the meantime, create your own team vision statement. No one is stopping you from becoming a powerful leader. Declaring a path with a destination is the first great step a leader can take.

List obstacles that your team members and leaders could encounter along the road. Include team personality types, and other challenges to be expected. What skills would be required to help them through the rubble? Having an open discussion about these anxieties will help your team prepare for both the expected and unexpected turbulence.

Activate positive attitudes through a reward system. Tackling defiant giants is a daunting task, but if you start in the defeat mode, you'll end up defeated. Remember, you're Tink, the great encourager. According to Teresa Aubele, PhD., Stan Wenck, EdD., and Susan Reynolds, who have done extensive research for their book, *Train Your Brain to Get Happy*, you can exercise your brain to bury negative energy by concentrating on positive thoughts. A happy brain produces a healthier life.

Never lose sight of your faith. Make it a habit to include God in every area of your life. Your journey is hard enough; there's no reason to go it alone. When your actions align with your purpose, He will protect and bless you. Continue to serve yourself with His love so you have the ability to serve others. Lead from your strongest point of access, the inside, and watch the outside become a magnet for success.

Encouraging positive attitudes in the work place is possible through great leadership. Don't miss it! Don't miss becoming number one in your company or division; let MMPP Leadership retreats make it happen!

THE NEW BEGINNING JOURNAL

The Momentum Factor

The Law of Value

Your true worth is determined by how much more you give in value

than you take in payment.

The Go-Giver

My hope was to bring you to a deeper understanding of leadership; how a leader can influence others and how a leader can change the course of employee engagement. Now that you've read this book, in your words, write what it means to be a leader.

_____

_____

_____

_____

_____

_____

What strengths do you bring to your team?

_____

_____

_____

_____

Great leadership focuses on the people you serve so the company is able to rise in production. The building blocks of momentum—purpose, direction, and trust—will determine the strength and influence of your leadership. Think about your personal story and how you can build trust by relaying a tale of triumph so others will be inspired.

_____

_____

_____

_____

_____

_____

_____

How will you build purpose into your life and how will this affect your leadership?

_____

_____

_____

_____

_____

_____

What is your ultimate goal this year as a team leader?

_____

_____

_____

_____

_____

What are your immediate little team 'wins' or goals to achieve along the way? Think of your team as a chess board and the goal as the 'check-mate.' Who has to move, and where, in order to reach the ultimate goal?

_____

_____

_____

_____

_____

_____

_____

_____

_____

Motivational incentives are small plays leaders initiate to maintain momentum. List a few game plans you can implement and the small tokens for the winners.

_____

_____

_____

_____

_____

_____

_____

Team members want to be included to help achieve a goal. How will you delegate the strengths of other team members so they feel a part of the project and a part of the ultimate win? What will you ask them to do?

_____

_____

_____

_____

_____

What time management strategies will you put in place to help organize your day? (Train on this during your next department or team meeting!)

_____

_____

_____

_____

_____

_____

What are you going to do less of in order to generate more work from more people on your team?

_____

_____

_____

_____

_____

_____

_____

_____

What shifts in your thinking and behavior will make the biggest impact on the acceleration of engagement with your team?

_____

_____

_____

_____

_____

_____

_____

When is your retreat scheduled?

_____

Congratulations! Momentum is brewing and you're on your way to a great leader-shift!

TAMILYN BANNO

ABOUT THE AUTHOR

Mastering leadership is about balance, momentum, and being centered on the people we serve.

Tamilyn Banno is a Thought Leader and mentor in personal and leadership development. Known for her inspirational leadership retreats and the Momentum Model of Leadership, she engages and produces highly proficient leaders and teams. Tami, as called by her family and friends, consults with other sales executives, managers, and entrepreneurs to help design, organize, and facilitate their own successful retreats.

Tami is also the author of *Authentic Purpose*, the *Authentic Purpose Workbook*, the *Leadership Activity Guide*, and *How to Host Your Own MomenTEAM Event*.

Made in the USA
Middletown, DE
30 January 2021